PENGUIN BUSINESS

THE ART OF CONVERSATION

Khurshed Dordi is a chief operating officer (COO) turned business and leadership coach. He was the managing director and group COO India at Deutsche Bank AG. Khurshed has over three decades of global experience in the financial services industry. He is also an educator for MBA students, a mentor and an internationally certified coach.

THE ART OF CONVERSATION

Elevate Your Communication Skills, Influence Outcomes and Connect with Anyone

Khurshed Dordi

PENGUIN
BUSINESS

An imprint of Penguin Random House

PENGUIN BUSINESS

Penguin Business is an imprint of the Penguin Random House group of companies
whose addresses can be found at global.penguinrandomhouse.com

Published by Penguin Random House India Pvt. Ltd
4th Floor, Capital Tower 1, MG Road,
Gurugram 122 002, Haryana, India

Penguin
Random House
India

First published in Penguin Business by Penguin Random House India 2025

ISBN 9780143476511

Typeset in League Spartan by Manipal Technologies Limited, Manipal
Printed at Thomson Press India Ltd, New Delhi

www.penguin.co.in

MIX
Paper | Supporting
responsible forestry
FSC® C010615

CONTENTS

Part III: Impactful Storytelling

Part IV: Integrating Skills in Daily Life

INTRODUCTION

'The most important conversations you'll ever have are the ones you have with yourself.' This quote, often attributed to the philosopher Plato, may seem a bit ironic as we delve into a book about mastering conversations with others. But the truth is that our internal dialogue shapes how we perceive the world and interact with those around us. It's the foundation upon which we build our confidence, our storytelling abilities and, ultimately, our professional success.

In today's fast-paced, interconnected world, where information flows freely and attention spans are fleeting, the ability to communicate effectively is more critical than ever. Yet so many of us struggle to articulate our thoughts clearly, connect with others authentically and leave a lasting impression. We stumble through awkward small talk, ramble during presentations and fail to tell compelling stories that resonate with our audience.

The good news is that communication is a skill, not an innate talent. And like any skill, it can be learnt, honed and mastered with practice and the right guidance. That's where this book comes in. We're not here to teach you a bunch of canned scripts or gimmicky tricks. Instead, we'll guide you through a holistic approach to communication that focuses on developing your inner strength, understanding the nuances of human interaction and crafting narratives that captivate and inspire.

Think of this book as your personal communication coach, trusted confidant and storytelling mentor—all rolled into one. We'll challenge you to step outside your comfort zone, confront your fears and embrace your unique voice. We'll equip you with the tools and techniques you need to navigate any conversation with poise and confidence, whether it's a job interview, client pitch or networking event. And we'll empower you to become a master storyteller, someone who can weave words into a tapestry of meaning and emotion, leaving a lasting impact on your listeners.

Why is storytelling so important, you might ask? Because stories are the currency of human connection. They're how we make sense of the world, share our experiences and build relationships. Stories have the power to move us, teach us and transform us. They can make us laugh, cry, think and act. In the professional realm, storytelling is an essential tool for persuasion, influence and leadership.

When you can tell a compelling story, you can sell your ideas, motivate your team and inspire your customers. You can create a shared vision, build a strong culture and drive innovation. Stories are the key to unlocking your full potential as a communicator, a leader and a professional.

But before we dive into the nitty-gritty of storytelling, let's first address the elephant in the room: confidence. Many of us struggle with self-doubt, imposter syndrome and the fear of public speaking. We worry about what others think of us, we second-guess our abilities and we shy away from opportunities to shine.

Confidence is not about being arrogant or brash. It's about believing in yourself, your worth and your potential. It's about knowing that you have something valuable to contribute and being willing to share it with the world. Confidence is the fuel that propels us forward, the spark that ignites our passion and the foundation upon which we build our success.

Throughout this book, we'll explore various techniques for building your confidence, from practising positive self-talk to visualizing success and celebrating your accomplishments. We'll also delve into the science of social anxiety and offer strategies for managing those butterflies in your stomach before a big presentation.

Remember, confidence is not a fixed trait. It's a muscle that can be strengthened with exercise and a mindset that can be cultivated with intention. The more you practise speaking up, sharing your ideas and taking risks, the more confident you'll become.

Of course, confidence alone is not enough. You also need to understand the dynamics of human interaction and the art of conversation. How do you build rapport with someone you've just met? How do you actively listen and respond empathetically? How do you handle difficult conversations with grace and tact? These are just a few of the questions we'll address in this book.

We'll also explore the power of non-verbal communication, from body language and facial expressions to tone of voice and eye contact. We'll discuss the importance of cultural sensitivity and how to adapt your communication style to different audiences. And we'll offer tips for navigating the digital landscape, where communication is often mediated through screens and keyboards.

PART I

THE ART OF
ASKING QUESTIONS

1

INTRODUCTION TO QUESTIONING

Asking questions is an essential skill in any conversation. It helps gather information, gain clarity and show interest in the other person. However, asking the right questions requires practice and understanding of different types of questions.

This section will cover the basics of questioning and how it can enhance your communication skills. We will also explore the power of open-ended and closed-ended questions and when to use them effectively.

In the complex dance of human interaction, a powerful tool exists that can unlock doors, forge connections and illuminate the path to understanding: the art of questioning. As Voltaire eloquently said, 'Judge a man by his questions rather than his answers.' Questions are not mere inquiries; they are catalysts for thought, sparks that ignite curiosity and pathways to deeper knowledge.

Some of human communication is non-verbal, a silent symphony of expressions, gestures and subtle cues. Yet, within the spoken word lies an extraordinary power to shape perception, influence outcomes and build rapport. And at the heart of this power lies the question.

Questions are not simply tools for gathering information; they are instruments of connection. When we ask a question, we extend an invitation—to share, engage and collaborate. We signal our interest, curiosity and willingness to learn. And in that exchange, we open a window into the minds and hearts of others.

But not all questions are created equal. Some questions are closed, seeking a simple yes or no answer. Others are open-ended, inviting exploration and elaboration. And still others are leading, subtly guiding the conversation towards a desired outcome. The most effective questions are those that are carefully crafted, thoughtfully delivered and genuinely curious. They are questions that challenge assumptions, spark new ideas and encourage deeper reflection.

In the realm of professional success, the art of questioning is an indispensable skill. Whether you're interviewing for a job, negotiating a deal or leading a team, the ability to ask the right questions can make all the difference. It can help you uncover hidden opportunities, build trust and rapport and create a culture of collaboration and innovation.

Take the example of a job interview. A well-prepared candidate will not only answer the interviewer's questions thoughtfully but will also ask insightful questions of their own. This demonstrates initiative, curiosity and a genuine interest in the role and company. It can also help the candidate assess whether the job is a good fit for their skills and aspirations.

In the world of sales, questions are the lifeblood of the relationship between the salesperson and the customer. By asking the right questions, a salesperson can uncover the customer's needs, pain points and motivations. This information is essential for tailoring the sales pitch and closing the deal.

However, the power of questioning extends far beyond the realms of interviews and sales. In any professional setting, the ability to ask the right questions can help you build relationships, influence outcomes and achieve your goals. It can help you gain a deeper understanding of your colleagues, customers and your industry. It can help you identify problems, develop solutions and drive innovation.

Questions are not just for the workplace, of course. They are essential tools for personal growth and development. When we ask ourselves questions, we challenge our assumptions, expand our perspectives and deepen our understanding of ourselves and the world around us.

But perhaps the most important questions we can ask are those that challenge us to think critically, question the status quo and envision a better future. These are the questions that drive innovation, inspire creativity and lead to positive change.

In the words of Albert Einstein, 'The important thing is not to stop questioning. Curiosity has its own reason for existing.' When we embrace the power of questioning, we open ourselves up to a world of possibilities. We expand our knowledge, deepen our understanding and forge stronger connections with others. And, in so doing, we unlock the full potential of human interaction.

The art of questioning is not simply a skill to be mastered; it is a way of life. It is a commitment to curiosity, a thirst for knowledge and a willingness to engage with the world around us. When we embrace the power of questioning, we embark on a journey of lifelong learning and discovery. And, in that journey, we find not only answers but also the inspiration to ask even more questions.

So, the next time you find yourself in a conversation, whether it's with a colleague, a customer or a loved one, remember the power of the question. Ask with curiosity, listen with intention and be open to the unexpected. For in the art of questioning lies the key to unlocking the full potential of human connection and achieving professional success.

The Importance of Questions

'Judge a man by his questions rather than his answers.'
—Voltaire

Renowned French philosopher Voltaire, with this simple yet profound statement, encapsulates the essence of questions—the power they hold in shaping thoughts, driving discovery and fostering understanding. In the grand scheme of communication, questions often take a backseat to answers.

We are conditioned to believe that answers signify knowledge, authority and perhaps even power. However, a paradigm shift is underway. The spotlight is now on the art of asking questions, the skill that fuels intellectual curiosity, ignites creativity and builds meaningful connections.

The Question as a Catalyst for Change

In an era overflowing with information, the ability to ask the right questions is a potent tool. Questions act as catalysts, propelling us beyond the surface level of knowledge to uncover deeper insights. They challenge assumptions, spark debate and invite a plurality of perspectives. In the realms of science, philosophy, business and personal development, questions are not merely tools for gathering information; they are instruments of transformation.

Consider the groundbreaking discoveries that have shaped our world—from Albert Einstein's theory of relativity to the development of the Internet. Each of these monumental achievements was born out of a simple question, a spark of curiosity that ignited a quest for knowledge. In a similar vein, businesses that foster a culture of inquiry are more likely to innovate and adapt to a rapidly changing landscape. By encouraging employees to question the status quo, companies create an environment where ideas flourish and solutions emerge.

The Question as a Bridge to Understanding

Questions are the threads that weave connections between individuals. They invite dialogue, foster empathy and build trust. When we ask questions, we demonstrate a genuine interest in others, their experiences and their perspectives. This act of curiosity creates a space for shared understanding and mutual respect.

Questions have the power to bridge the gaps between us. By seeking to understand rather than to judge, we open the door to dialogue and collaboration. Questions invite us to step outside our echo chambers and engage with those who hold different beliefs and values. In this way, questions become a force for unity and reconciliation.

The Question as a Tool for Personal Growth

The act of asking questions is not only a means of connecting with others; it is also a pathway to self-discovery. When we question our assumptions, we challenge our own biases and broaden our perspectives. We become more open-minded, more empathetic and more willing to learn.

Questions are powerful tools for self-reflection and growth. By asking ourselves probing questions about our values, goals and motivations, we gain clarity and direction. We can identify our strengths and weaknesses, and we are empowered to make positive changes in our lives.

The Question as a Source of Joy

The joy of asking questions is not limited to intellectual pursuits or personal growth. Questions can also be a source of amusement, entertainment and wonder. From playful riddles to philosophical inquiries, questions have the power to spark our imaginations and ignite our sense of curiosity.

Questions are often used to evoke emotions, challenge norms and provoke thought. They invite us to question our assumptions about the world and to explore new possibilities. In this way, questions can be a source of inspiration and creativity.

The importance of questions cannot be overstated. They are the keys that unlock the doors of knowledge, understanding and connection. They are the catalysts that spark change, the bridges that build relationships and the tools that empower personal growth. As we navigate an ever-changing world, let us embrace the power of inquiry and allow questions to guide us on our journey of lifelong learning and discovery.

Types of Questions: Open vs Closed

Each path serves a unique purpose, guiding us towards different destinations in the pursuit of knowledge, understanding and connection.

Open-Ended Questions: The Gateway to Exploration

Open-ended questions are the adventurers of the questioning world. They are not confined by simple 'yes' and 'no' answers but rather invite expansive responses, encouraging exploration, elaboration and the sharing of thoughts, feelings and perspectives. These questions often begin with words like 'why', 'how' or 'what if', opening the door to a world of possibilities.

Consider the question, 'What are your thoughts on the future of artificial intelligence?' This open-ended invitation allows the respondent to delve into their personal beliefs, concerns and hopes, sparking a conversation that could lead to new insights, shared passions or even collaborative endeavours.

Open-ended questions are particularly valuable in situations where you seek to:

- **Uncover Deeper Insights:** By inviting individuals to share their unique perspectives and experiences, open-ended questions can reveal hidden motivations, underlying beliefs and nuanced understandings that would otherwise remain obscured.
- **Foster Connection and Understanding:** Open-ended questions create a space for authentic dialogue, where individuals feel heard, valued and understood. This can strengthen relationships, build trust and foster a sense of connection.
- **Stimulate Creativity and Innovation:** By encouraging individuals to think beyond the confines of predetermined answers, open-ended questions can spark new ideas, challenge assumptions and lead to innovative solutions.
- **Gather Qualitative Data:** Open-ended questions can provide rich, detailed information that cannot be captured through closed-ended questions. This

type of data is often invaluable in research, customer feedback and other contexts, where understanding the 'why' behind an answer is crucial.

However, open-ended questions are not without their drawbacks. They can be time-consuming, requiring more effort from both the questioner and the respondent. They can also lead to rambling or tangential responses, making it difficult to extract the desired information. Therefore, it's important to use open-ended questions strategically, choosing the right time and place to maximize their impact.

Closed-Ended Questions: The Compass of Confirmation

Closed-ended questions are the navigators of the questioning world. They provide clear direction, seeking specific information, confirmation or clarification. These questions often elicit brief responses, such as 'yes' or 'no', or a single word or phrase.

Consider the question, 'Do you agree with the proposed changes to the company policy?' This closed-ended question seeks a clear, concise answer, allowing you to quickly gauge the respondent's stance on the issue.

Closed-ended questions are particularly useful in situations where you seek to:

- **Confirm Understanding:** By asking questions that require simple 'yes' or 'no' answers, you can ensure that the respondent has understood your message or instructions correctly.
- **Clarify Details:** Closed-ended questions can help you obtain specific information, such as dates, times or quantities.
- **Make Decisions:** By asking questions that require the respondent to choose between two or more options, you can gather the information needed to make informed decisions.
- **Gather Quantitative Data:** Closed-ended questions are ideal for collecting data that can be easily measured and analysed, such as demographics or preferences.

However, closed-ended questions can also be limiting, preventing the respondent from sharing additional information or insights. They can also come across as interrogative or leading, creating a sense of pressure or discomfort. Therefore, it's important to use closed-ended questions judiciously, balancing their efficiency with the need for openness and exploration.

The Art of Balancing Open and Closed Questions

The most effective questioners understand the art of balancing open and closed questions. They recognize that each type of question serves a distinct purpose, and they use them strategically to achieve their desired outcomes.

For example, you might begin a conversation with open-ended questions to build rapport, explore interests and uncover underlying motivations. Once you have established a connection, you can then use closed-ended questions to gather specific information, confirm understanding and make decisions.

The key is to be adaptable and responsive, adjusting your questioning style to fit the situation and the individual. By mastering the art of balancing open and closed questions, you can unlock the full potential of inquiry, leading to deeper insights, stronger connections and more meaningful conversations.

The Socratic Method

> *'I cannot teach anybody anything, I can only make them think.'*
>
> —Socrates

In the realm of intellectual discourse and critical thinking, few tools rival the potency and enduring influence of the Socratic Method. Born from the mind of the enigmatic Greek philosopher Socrates, this method is an intricate dance of questions and answers designed to dismantle assumptions, expose contradictions and illuminate deeper truths. Its legacy stretches across millennia, permeating fields from philosophy and law to education and everyday conversations.

Unveiling the Essence of the Socratic Method

At its core, the Socratic Method is a dynamic process of inquiry. It eschews the traditional model of passive learning, where knowledge is simply transmitted from teacher to student. Instead, it fosters active engagement, inviting participants to become co-creators in their own understanding. The 'teacher' in this context is less an instructor and more a facilitator, skilfully guiding the conversation with a series of carefully crafted questions.

The heart of the Socratic Method lies in its emphasis on questions rather than answers. These questions are not mere requests for information but rather tools for exploration. They are open-ended, probing and often challenge the very foundations of the respondent's beliefs. This process of questioning is known as 'elenchus', and it is the driving force behind the Socratic dialogue.

The Artful Dance of Questioning

The Socratic Method is not a haphazard barrage of inquiries. It is a meticulously orchestrated sequence designed to lead the respondent on a journey of self-discovery. The questions begin broad and gradually become more specific, homing in on the inconsistencies and contradictions within the respondent's thought process.

One common technique employed in the Socratic Method is the use of 'maieutics', or intellectual midwifery. Just as a midwife helps a mother give birth to a child, the Socratic questioner helps the respondent give birth to their own ideas. This is done through a series of gentle but persistent questions that encourage the respondent to clarify their thoughts, examine their assumptions and ultimately arrive at their own conclusions.

Another hallmark of the Socratic Method is its emphasis on humility and intellectual honesty. Socrates himself famously claimed to know nothing, and this attitude of open-mindedness and willingness to be proven wrong is central to the Socratic dialogue. The goal is not to win an argument but to arrive at a deeper understanding of the truth.

The Impact of the Socratic Method

The Socratic Method is not merely an academic exercise. It has profound implications for how we think, learn and interact with the world around us. By encouraging us to question our assumptions and examine our beliefs, it cultivates critical thinking skills that are essential for navigating the complexities of modern life.

In the field of education, the Socratic Method is a powerful tool for fostering intellectual curiosity and independent thinking. Encouraging students to actively participate in their own learning helps them develop a deeper understanding of the subject matter and a greater appreciation for the power of ideas.

In the realm of law, the Socratic Method is a cornerstone of legal education. Law students are routinely grilled by their professors in a process known as the 'Socratic Method of teaching'. This method helps students develop the analytical and argumentation skills that are essential for success in the legal profession.

Beyond its formal applications, the Socratic Method can also be a valuable tool for personal growth and self-discovery. By engaging in Socratic dialogues with ourselves or others, we can gain a deeper understanding of our own beliefs, values and motivations. This can lead to greater self-awareness, improved decision-making and a more fulfilling life.

The Socratic Method in the Modern World

In an era of information overload and echo chambers, the Socratic Method is more relevant than ever. It offers a way to cut through the noise and get to the heart of the matter. By encouraging us to question everything, it helps us develop a healthy scepticism that is essential for discerning truth from falsehood.

The Socratic Method is not without its critics. Some argue that it can be used to manipulate and confuse others. However, when used in good faith, it is a powerful tool for intellectual exploration and personal growth.

The Socratic Method is a timeless tool that has the power to transform the way we think, learn and interact with the world. By embracing the art of asking questions, we can unlock our full intellectual potential and become active participants in our own understanding.

As we continue to navigate the complexities of the modern world, the Socratic Method offers a beacon of hope, reminding us that the pursuit of knowledge is an ongoing journey of inquiry and self-discovery. By embracing this method, we can cultivate a lifelong love of learning and a deeper appreciation for the power of ideas.

2

TECHNIQUES FOR EFFECTIVE QUESTIONING

Asking questions is an essential part of communication and can greatly impact the outcome of a conversation. Effective questioning techniques can help to gather information, clarify misunderstandings or challenge assumptions. In this section, we will discuss some techniques that you can use to ask questions effectively.

Active Listening and Its Role

'We have two ears and one mouth so that we can listen twice as much as we speak.'

—Epictetus

This timeless wisdom from the Stoic philosopher Epictetus underscores a fundamental truth about human communication: effective questioning hinges on active listening. In the dynamic exchange of questions and answers, listening isn't merely a passive act; it's an engaged, intentional process that lays the groundwork for insightful inquiry.

The Art of Active Listening

Active listening is more than simply hearing the words spoken; it's about immersing oneself in the speaker's message, both verbal and non-verbal. It involves paying attention to not just the content of the words, but also the tone, inflection, facial expressions and body language that accompany them. This holistic approach allows you to discern the underlying emotions, motivations and nuances that enrich the conversation.

One of the hallmarks of active listening is the ability to give the speaker your undivided attention. This means putting aside distractions, resisting the urge to formulate your response while the speaker is still talking and focusing on truly understanding their perspective. It's about creating a space where the speaker feels heard, valued and understood.

The Benefits of Active Listening

The benefits of active listening are far-reaching and profound. In the context of effective questioning, active listening catalyses deeper understanding, insightful inquiry and meaningful dialogue.

- **Building Rapport and Trust:** Active listening fosters a sense of connection and rapport between the questioner and the respondent. When people feel heard and understood, they are more likely to open up, share their thoughts and feelings and engage in authentic conversation. This trust is essential for eliciting honest and meaningful responses to your questions.
- **Uncovering Hidden Information:** Active listening enables you to glean insights that might not be explicitly stated. By paying attention to the speaker's non-verbal cues and subtle nuances, you can uncover hidden information, unspoken concerns and underlying motivations. This deeper understanding allows you to frame your questions in a way that elicits more comprehensive and relevant information.
- **Identifying Areas of Confusion or Misunderstanding:** Active listening helps you pinpoint areas where the speaker might be confused, uncertain or misinformed. By acknowledging and addressing these areas, you

can ensure that the conversation stays on track, clarify any misunderstandings and delve deeper into the topic at hand.

- **Crafting More Targeted and Relevant Questions:** Active listening informs your questioning strategy. By understanding the speaker's perspective, you can tailor your questions to their specific needs, interests and level of understanding. This ensures that your questions are relevant, targeted and elicit the most valuable information possible.

Techniques for Active Listening

Active listening is a skill that can be cultivated and honed through practice. Here are some techniques that can help you become a more effective active listener:

- **Maintain Eye Contact:** Making eye contact with the speaker demonstrates that you are engaged and interested in what they have to say. It also allows you to observe their non-verbal cues, which can provide valuable insights into their thoughts and feelings.
- **Use Encouraging Non-Verbal Cues:** Nodding your head, leaning forward slightly and maintaining an open and receptive posture all signal to the speaker that you are actively listening and encourages them to continue sharing.

- **Paraphrase and Summarize:** Periodically restating the speaker's message in your own words helps ensure that you have understood their message correctly. It also demonstrates your attentiveness and allows the speaker to clarify or elaborate on their points.
- **Ask Clarifying Questions:** If you are unsure about something the speaker has said, don't hesitate to ask for clarification. This shows your commitment to understanding their perspective and can lead to deeper insights and more meaningful conversations.
- **Avoid Interrupting:** Interrupting the speaker disrupts the flow of the conversation and can make them feel unheard and disrespected. Wait until they have finished speaking before offering your own thoughts or questions.
- **Be Patient and Allow for Silence:** Sometimes, the most powerful moments in a conversation occur during pauses and silences. Don't rush to fill the silence; allow the speaker time to gather their thoughts and express themselves fully.
- **Be Empathetic:** Empathy is the ability to understand and share the feelings of another person. By putting yourself in the speaker's shoes, you can better understand their perspective, motivations and concerns. This understanding can inform your questions and lead to more meaningful dialogue.

Active listening is a skill that can be learnt and improved with practice. There are many resources available, including books, articles and workshops, that can help individuals develop their active listening skills. By investing time and effort in developing this skill, individuals can enhance their communication, build stronger relationships and achieve greater success in all aspects of life.

Active listening is a powerful tool for effective communication and building strong relationships. It's a skill that requires effort and focus, but the rewards are immeasurable. By actively listening to others, we can gain a deeper understanding of their perspectives, build trust and rapport and create a more positive and productive environment for everyone.

Framing Your Questions

'The difference between the right word and the almost right word is the difference between lightning and the lightning bug.'

—Mark Twain

Twain's words ring especially true when it comes to the art of questioning. The questions we pose, much like the words we choose, can illuminate, obfuscate or even mislead. In the realm of effective questioning, framing is not merely a stylistic flourish; it is the bedrock upon which meaningful dialogue is built.

The Architecture of a Question

A question, at its core, is a linguistic structure designed to elicit information. However, beneath this simple definition lies a nuanced architecture comprising several key elements:

- **The Interrogative:** This is the grammatical form that signals a question—words like 'who', 'what', 'where', 'when', 'why' and 'how'. The interrogative sets the stage, indicating the type of information being sought.
- **The Presupposition:** This is the underlying assumption embedded within the question. For instance, the question 'Why are you late?' presupposes that the person is indeed late. Presuppositions can subtly influence the direction of a conversation.
- **The Focus:** This is the specific aspect of the topic that the question emphasizes. In the question, 'What are the potential risks of this project?', the focus is on the risks, not the benefits or other aspects.
- **The Tone:** This refers to the emotional quality of the question, which can range from neutral to accusatory, curious to sceptical. Tone can significantly impact the respondent's willingness to engage.

The Power of Framing

The way we frame our questions, by manipulating these elements, can profoundly impact the responses we receive. Consider the following examples:

- **Example 1:** 'Are you satisfied with your current salary?' (Neutral tone, focus on satisfaction)
- **Example 2:** 'Don't you think you deserve a raise?' (Accusatory tone, presupposes dissatisfaction)

While both questions inquire about the respondent's feelings regarding their salary, the framing is vastly different. The first question is open-ended and invites a nuanced response, while the second is leading and suggests a specific answer.

The Spectrum of Question Types

Questions are not monolithic; they exist on a spectrum, each type serving a distinct purpose:

- **Open Questions:** These questions invite expansive answers and encourage the respondent to share their thoughts and feelings freely. They often begin with 'what', 'how' or 'why'.
- **Closed Questions:** These questions seek specific information and typically elicit short, factual

responses. They often begin with 'who', 'where', 'when' or 'did'.

- **Leading Questions:** These questions suggest a particular answer and can be used to confirm or challenge assumptions. They often contain phrases like 'don't you think' or 'wouldn't you agree'.
- **Probing Questions:** These questions delve deeper into a topic, seeking clarification or elaboration. They often follow up on previous responses and can help uncover hidden information.
- **Rhetorical Questions:** These questions are not meant to be answered but rather to make a point or provoke thought.

Framing for Specific Outcomes

The art of framing lies in selecting the right type of question for the desired outcome. Here are some strategies for achieving specific objectives:

- **To Encourage Openness:** Use open questions that invite the respondent to share their thoughts and feelings. Avoid leading questions or judgmental language.
- **To Gather Specific Information:** Use closed questions that focus on the desired details. Be clear and concise in your wording.

- **To Challenge Assumptions:** Use leading questions to expose potential biases or inconsistencies. Be respectful and avoid personal attacks.
- **To Deepen Understanding:** Use probing questions to explore nuances and uncover hidden information. Be curious and attentive to the respondent's answers.
- **To Spark Reflection:** Use rhetorical questions to provoke thought and stimulate discussion. Be mindful of the context and avoid excessive use.

The Ethical Dimension of Framing

While framing can be a powerful tool, it is essential to wield it ethically. Avoid manipulating questions to deceive or coerce. Respect the respondent's autonomy and strive for genuine dialogue.

Framing is only half the equation; the other half is listening. Actively listen to the respondent's answers, paying attention to both verbal and non-verbal cues. This will help you tailor your subsequent questions and maintain a productive dialogue.

Framing as a Lifelong Skill

Mastering the art of framing takes time and practice. It is a lifelong skill that can be honed through continuous learning and self-reflection. By paying attention to how others frame their questions and by experimenting with different approaches, you can gradually develop your own unique style.

The art of framing your questions is a multifaceted skill that involves understanding the architecture of a question, utilizing different question types and tailoring your approach to specific outcomes. By approaching questioning with intentionality and ethical considerations, you can foster meaningful dialogue, deepen understanding and achieve your communication goals.

Timing and Context

'Ask the right question at the right time.'

This simple yet profound maxim underpins the art of effective questioning. In the intricate dance of communication, timing and context act as the choreographer, guiding the rhythm and flow of dialogue. Just as a well-timed musical note can evoke powerful emotions, a well-placed question, delivered within the appropriate context, can unlock deep insights, stimulate critical thinking and foster meaningful connections.

The Symphony of Timing

Timing is a multifaceted element in the realm of questioning. It involves not only the chronological moment when a question is posed but also the psychological and emotional readiness of both the questioner and the respondent. A premature question can fall flat, while a delayed one can miss its mark entirely.

Consider the scenario of a teacher introducing a complex concept to a group of students. If the teacher were to launch into a barrage of questions before allowing the students time to process the information, the questions would likely be met with confusion and frustration. Conversely, if the teacher waited too long to engage the students, their attention might wane and the opportunity for active learning could be lost.

The skilled questioner possesses an intuitive sense of timing, honed through experience and observation. They can discern when a moment of silence is needed to allow for reflection, when a light-hearted question can diffuse tension or when a probing inquiry can delve deeper into a topic.

The Landscape of Context

Context encompasses the circumstances, environment and background knowledge that shape the meaning and relevance of a question. It includes factors such as the relationship between the questioner and the respondent, the purpose of the dialogue and the cultural norms that govern communication.

Imagine a job interview where the interviewer asks a candidate about their personal life. If the question is posed within the context of assessing the candidate's ability to maintain work-life balance, it might be considered appropriate. However, if the same question is asked in a way that suggests discriminatory intent, it would be highly inappropriate.

The adept questioner takes the time to understand the context in which a question will be received. They consider the cultural sensitivities of the audience, the power dynamics at play and the overall objectives of the conversation. By doing so, they ensure that their questions are not only relevant but also respectful and culturally sensitive.

The Interplay of Timing and Context

Timing and context are not isolated elements; they are intertwined in a dynamic relationship. The appropriateness of a question's timing can depend heavily on the context, and vice versa.

For instance, a question about a sensitive topic might be perfectly acceptable among close friends but entirely out of place in a professional setting. Similarly, a question that is well-received in a casual conversation might be perceived as intrusive or inappropriate in a formal interview.

The interplay of timing and context is particularly evident in the realm of feedback. Constructive criticism, when delivered at the right time and in the right way, can be a powerful tool for growth and development.

However, if the same feedback is offered prematurely or in a harsh or judgemental manner, it can be demoralizing and counterproductive.

Mastering the Art of Timing and Context

Developing mastery over the nuances of timing and context requires a combination of knowledge, skill and intuition. It involves learning the principles of effective communication, practising active listening and cultivating empathy and emotional intelligence.

Active listening is a crucial component of this mastery. By paying close attention to both verbal and non-verbal cues, the questioner can gain valuable insights into the respondent's state of mind, emotional readiness and understanding of the topic at hand. This information can then be used to tailor questions in a way that is both timely and relevant.

Empathy and emotional intelligence are equally important. By putting themselves in the respondent's shoes, the questioner can anticipate how their questions will be received and adjust their approach accordingly. This ability to connect with others on an emotional level is essential for building trust and rapport, which are essential for effective communication.

Timing and context are not mere technicalities in the art of questioning; they are the very essence of effective communication. By understanding the nuances of these two elements and honing their skills through practice and reflection, questioners can unlock the full potential of their questions, fostering deeper understanding, stimulating critical thinking and building stronger relationships.

3

QUESTIONING IN
DIFFERENT CONTEXTS

Questioning is a fundamental aspect of communication and learning. It involves asking for information, clarifying ideas and challenging assumptions to gain a deeper understanding. Questioning can take place in various contexts, personal relationships, professional settings and social interactions. In this section, we will discuss the role and importance of questioning in different contexts.

Personal Relationships

'The most powerful conversations are often the ones we have with ourselves.'

In the intricate ballet of personal relationships, communication is the music that guides our steps. And within this symphony, questioning plays a melody both subtle and profound. Yet, questioning in the personal sphere isn't merely about seeking information—it's a tool for connection, growth and understanding.

The Spectrum of Inquiry

From the innocent curiosity of a child's 'why?' to the probing introspection of a therapist's 'tell me more', questions in personal relationships span a wide spectrum. They can be:

- **Clarifying:** 'When you said "later", did you mean this evening or tomorrow?'
- **Probing:** 'What led you to feel that way about the situation?'
- **Inviting:** 'Would you like to share your thoughts on this?'
- **Challenging:** 'Do you think that's the only way to view it?'

Each type of question serves a distinct purpose, and the artistry lies in choosing the right one at the right moment.

The Unseen Power of Questions

Beyond their surface function, questions in personal relationships wield a subtler power. They can:

- **Build Intimacy:** By showing genuine interest in another's thoughts and feelings, we foster closeness and trust.
- **Spark Reflection:** Thought-provoking questions can lead to personal growth and self-discovery.
- **Resolve Conflict:** Skilful questioning can help uncover underlying issues and pave the way for resolution.
- **Express Care:** A simple 'How are you feeling?' can communicate empathy and support.
- **Set Boundaries:** Assertive questions can clarify expectations and prevent misunderstandings.

In essence, questions are not just a means to an end; they are a force that shapes the dynamics of our interactions.

The Art of Questioning

Like any art form, questioning in personal relationships requires finesse and intention. It's not just about what we ask but how we ask. Consider the following:

- **Tone:** A gentle, curious tone invites openness, while an accusatory one breeds defensiveness.

- **Timing:** Choosing the right moment to ask a sensitive question can make all the difference.
- **Motivation:** Are you asking to understand, to connect or to manipulate? Your intention influences the impact of your question.
- **Listening:** True questioning involves active listening, not just waiting for your turn to speak.

Mastering the art of questioning takes practice and self-awareness, but the rewards are immeasurable.

Questioning in Different Relationship Contexts

The way we question varies depending on the relationship context. With a romantic partner, our questions may be more intimate and vulnerable. With a friend, we might be more playful and spontaneous. With a family member, our questions might be shaped by shared history and dynamics.

Understanding these nuances allows us to tailor our questions to the specific needs of each relationship.

Questioning Ourselves

In personal relationships, the most important questions we ask may be directed inward: 'What do I truly want from this relationship?' or 'How am I contributing to the dynamic?' or 'What am I afraid to ask?'

By honestly examining our own motivations and fears, we gain clarity and agency in our interactions.

The Ongoing Dialogue

Questioning in personal relationships is not a static act but an ongoing dialogue. As relationships evolve, so do our questions. We learn, we grow and we adapt. By embracing the interrogative dance, we open ourselves to a deeper connection, greater understanding and a more fulfilling relational journey.

Professional Settings

'The important thing is not to stop questioning.
Curiosity has its own reason for existing.'
—Albert Einstein

In the bustling heart of professional life, where decisions carry weight and interactions shape outcomes, the ability to ask effective questions emerges as an indispensable skill. It's a tool that unlocks understanding, fosters collaboration and propels innovation. Drawing inspiration from the concept of 'Questioning in Different Contexts', this chapter delves into the nuanced art of inquiry within the professional sphere.

The Power of Questions in the Workplace

Questions are not mere interrogations; they are catalysts for progress. In a professional setting, the right question can illuminate a complex issue, challenge assumptions or spark a creative solution. A well-placed question can also build rapport, demonstrate active listening and cultivate a culture of curiosity.

Consider the impact of a simple question like, 'What challenges are we facing in this project?' This seemingly innocuous inquiry can uncover hidden obstacles, encourage team members to voice concerns and ultimately lead to a more robust project plan.

Types of Questions for Professional Success

Not all questions are created equal. In the professional context, different types of questions serve distinct purposes:

- **Clarifying Questions:** These seek to eliminate ambiguity and ensure a shared understanding. Examples include, 'Could you elaborate on that point?' or 'What do you mean by [term]?'
- **Probing Questions:** These delve deeper into a topic, uncovering underlying motivations or assumptions. Examples include, 'What factors led you to that

conclusion?' or 'Can you provide an example of how that would work?'

- **Hypothetical Questions:** These explore possibilities and encourage creative thinking. Examples include, 'What if we approached this problem from a different angle?' or 'How would this solution impact our stakeholders?'
- **Reflective Questions:** These invite introspection and encourage a deeper understanding of a situation. Examples include, 'What have we learnt from this experience?' or 'How can we apply these insights moving forward?'

Tailoring Questions to Different Professional Interactions

The art of questioning extends beyond selecting the right type of question. It also involves adapting your approach to different professional interactions:

- **Meetings:** Questions in meetings can foster engagement, encourage participation and drive decision-making. Consider asking open-ended questions that invite diverse perspectives.
- **Presentations:** Questions during or after presentations can clarify information, demonstrate interest and provide valuable feedback. Be respectful and concise in your inquiries.

- **Networking:** Questions in networking settings can help you build rapport, gather information and identify potential opportunities. Focus on questions that show genuine interest in the other person.
- **Negotiations:** Questions in negotiations can help you understand the other party's needs, uncover potential compromises and reach mutually beneficial agreements. Ask probing questions to reveal underlying motivations.

Overcoming Challenges to Effective Questioning

Despite the power of questions, several challenges can hinder their effectiveness in the professional arena:

- **Fear of Appearing Uninformed:** Some professionals hesitate to ask questions for fear of revealing a lack of knowledge. However, asking for clarification is often a sign of intellectual curiosity and a willingness to learn.
- **Time Constraints:** In fast-paced professional environments, time is a precious commodity. However, taking a few moments to ask thoughtful questions can save time in the long run by preventing misunderstandings and ensuring that everyone is on the same page.
- **Power dynamics:** In hierarchical organizations, power imbalances can discourage individuals from

asking questions of their superiors. However, creating a culture of open communication where questions are valued can mitigate this challenge.

Cultivating a Questioning Mindset

To become a master of inquiry in the professional realm, cultivate a questioning mindset:

- **Embrace Curiosity:** Be genuinely interested in learning new things and understanding different perspectives.
- **Challenge Assumptions:** Don't take information at face value. Question the status quo and explore alternative possibilities.
- **Listen Actively:** Pay attention to what others are saying, both verbally and non-verbally. Ask clarifying questions to ensure that you understand their message.
- **Be Open to Feedback:** Be willing to receive feedback on your questions and adjust your approach accordingly.
- **Practise Regularly:** The more you ask questions, the more comfortable and skilled you will become. Seek out opportunities to ask questions in a variety of professional settings.

Questions are the threads that connect us to knowledge, understanding and innovation. By mastering the art of inquiry, we unlock our full potential as professionals and contribute to a more collaborative, creative and successful workplace.

Social Interactions

'We are caught in an inescapable network of mutuality, tied in a single garment of destiny. Whatever affects one directly, affects all indirectly.'

—Martin Luther King Jr

These words from the iconic civil rights leader encapsulate the essence of social interaction—a complex ballet of connection, communication and mutual influence that underpins human existence. In this chapter, we embark on a journey to explore the intricacies of social interactions, peeling back the layers of this multifaceted phenomenon through the lens of inquiry. We'll delve into the diverse landscapes where social interactions unfold, from intimate conversations to bustling city streets, and scrutinize the questions that arise at each turn.

The Ever-Present Symphony

Social interaction isn't merely an occasional occurrence; it's a constant symphony playing in the background of our lives. From the moment we wake up to the time we drift off to sleep, we're immersed in a web of interactions, both overt and subtle. The morning greeting exchanged with a family member, the non-verbal cues shared during a business meeting, the shared laughter with friends—these are all notes in the composition of our social existence.

Let's pause and ask: What makes a social interaction truly meaningful? Is it the depth of the conversation, the shared experience or simply the feeling of being seen and heard by another? The answers to these questions vary from person to person, highlighting the subjective nature of social engagement.

Contexts of Connection

Social interactions are not confined to a single setting; they thrive in a multitude of contexts. Consider the intimate setting of a family dinner, where stories are shared, bonds are strengthened and traditions are upheld. Contrast this with the bustling energy of a city square, where strangers cross paths, conversations spark and a sense of collective energy emerges. Each context brings its unique flavour to the dance of connection.

The digital realm has added another layer to the tapestry of social interaction. Online platforms, social media networks and virtual communities have transformed the way we connect, communicate and build relationships.

While the digital landscape offers unprecedented opportunities for interaction, it also raises questions about the authenticity of online connections and the impact of screen-mediated communication on our social skills.

Unmasking Hidden Dynamics

Beneath the surface of every social interaction lies a myriad of hidden dynamics. Power struggles, social norms, cultural expectations and individual motivations all play a role in shaping how we interact with others. Consider a workplace meeting, where unspoken hierarchies influence who speaks up, who listens and whose ideas are ultimately heard. Or observe a group of friends navigating a disagreement, where conflicting values and loyalties come into play.

Inquiry allows us to peel back the layers of these hidden dynamics. By asking probing questions, we can uncover the unspoken rules that govern social behaviour and the motivations that drive individual actions. This process of unmasking can lead to greater self-awareness, empathy for others and a deeper understanding of the social forces at play.

The Art of Questioning

In social interaction, questions serve as powerful tools for exploration and understanding. They invite others to share their thoughts, feelings and experiences, fostering a sense of connection and mutual respect. The art of questioning involves more than just asking the right questions; it's about creating a safe and open space for dialogue, listening attentively to the responses and being willing to challenge our own assumptions.

Consider the impact of a simple question like, 'How are you feeling today?' This question can open the door to a meaningful conversation, allowing someone to express their emotions and feel heard. In a professional setting, a question like, 'What challenges are you facing in this project?' can spark a collaborative problem-solving session and lead to innovative solutions.

Beyond Words: The Language of Non-Verbal Cues

Social interaction is not solely about words; it's also about the intricate language of non-verbal cues. Facial expressions, body language, tone of voice and even the use of personal space all contribute to the messages we convey and receive. These non-verbal signals often speak louder than words, revealing underlying emotions, intentions and attitudes.

Think about a job interview, where a candidate's nervous fidgeting or confident handshake can significantly impact the interviewer's impression. Or observe a couple engaged in a heated argument, where their clenched fists and raised voices communicate anger and frustration more effectively than any words they might exchange.

Navigating Conflict and Building Bridges

Conflict is an inevitable part of social interaction. Differences in opinions, values and goals can lead to misunderstandings, disagreements and even full-blown conflicts. However, conflict doesn't have to be destructive; it can also be an opportunity for growth, learning and deeper understanding.

The way we navigate conflict often depends on our communication skills, our willingness to compromise and our ability to see things from another's perspective. By asking open-ended questions, actively listening to the other person's concerns and seeking common ground, we can transform conflict into a catalyst for positive change.

The Ripple Effect of Kindness

One of the most profound aspects of social interaction is the ripple effect of kindness. A simple act of generosity, compassion or understanding can have a cascading impact, spreading positivity and goodwill throughout a community. Conversely, acts of aggression, discrimination or disrespect can create a ripple effect of negativity, perpetuating conflict and division.

This highlights the power of our individual choices in shaping the social fabric of our world. By choosing kindness, empathy and respect in our interactions with others, we contribute to a more harmonious and interconnected society.

Embracing Diversity, Fostering Inclusion

Social interactions are enriched by diversity. When we engage with people from different backgrounds, cultures and perspectives, we broaden our horizons, challenge our assumptions and gain a deeper understanding of the human experience. Embracing diversity and fostering inclusion in our social interactions is not only a moral imperative; it's also a key to unlocking our collective potential.

This involves actively seeking out diverse perspectives, listening with an open mind and valuing the unique contributions that each individual brings to the table. By creating inclusive spaces where everyone feels safe to express themselves authentically, we cultivate a vibrant tapestry of human connection.

4

DEEPENING CONVERSATIONS

When it comes to having meaningful and engaging conversations, simply scratching the surface with small talk is not enough. To truly deepen a conversation and connect with someone on a deeper level, certain techniques and strategies can be employed.

One way to deepen a conversation is by adding follow-up questions or comments. This shows the person you are talking with that you are genuinely interested in what they have to say and want to learn more. Instead of just asking generic questions, try to ask specific follow-up questions related to the topic at hand. This not only keeps the conversation going but also allows for a deeper exploration of ideas and thoughts.

In this section, we will discuss some other ways to deepen conversations and make them more meaningful.

Follow-Up Questions

Conversations are the lifeblood of relationships, whether personal or professional. A well-placed question can unlock hidden insights, foster deeper connections and even spark innovation. Yet, so often, we find ourselves stuck in shallow exchanges, leaving much unsaid and unexplored. The key to unlocking deeper conversations lies in the art of follow-up questions.

The Power of Curiosity

Children are naturally curious, constantly asking 'Why?' and 'How?' Somewhere along the line, many of us lose this innate curiosity, content with surface-level understanding. But reigniting this spark can be transformative. Curiosity is the engine that drives meaningful conversations. It allows us to delve beneath the surface, uncover hidden layers and truly understand the perspectives of others. Follow-up questions are the fuel for this engine.

Consider a typical networking event. You meet someone new, exchange pleasantries and discuss your respective professions. Then, the conversation stalls. You feel like you've learnt the basics but haven't truly connected. This is where a well-crafted follow-up question can change the trajectory of the interaction. Instead of asking, 'What do you do?', try 'What's the most exciting project you're working on right now?' or 'What drew you to this field in the first place?' These questions invite the other person to share their passions, experiences and insights, leading to a far richer conversation.

Effective follow-up questions are not scripted or generic. They are born from active listening. When we truly listen, we pay attention not only to the words being spoken but also to the underlying emotions, motivations and nuances. We notice what is said and what is left unsaid. This attentiveness allows us to formulate follow-up questions that are relevant, insightful and respectful.

Types of Follow-Up Questions

There is no one-size-fits-all approach to follow-up questions. The right question depends on the context, relationship and desired outcome of the conversation. However, certain types of questions are particularly effective at deepening conversations:

- **Open-Ended Questions:** These questions cannot be answered with a simple 'yes' or 'no'. They invite elaboration, storytelling and the sharing of personal experiences. Examples include, 'Tell me more about that', 'What was that like for you?' and 'How did that make you feel?'

- **Clarifying Questions:** These questions seek to ensure understanding and avoid misinterpretations. They often begin with phrases like, 'Can you elaborate on that?', 'Could you give me an example?' or 'What do you mean by that?'

- **Probing Questions:** These questions delve deeper into a particular topic or idea. They can be used to uncover underlying motivations, challenge assumptions or explore complex issues. Examples include, 'Why do you think that is?', 'What led you to that conclusion?' and 'What are the implications of that?'

- **Reflective Questions:** These questions restate or summarize what the speaker has said, demonstrating active listening and ensuring mutual understanding. They often begin with phrases like, 'So, what you're saying is . . .', 'If I understand you correctly . . .', or 'Let me see if I've got this right . . .'

The Benefits of Follow-Up Questions

The art of follow-up questions is a powerful tool for personal and professional growth. By deepening conversations, we unlock a myriad of benefits:

- **Stronger Relationships:** Follow-up questions foster intimacy, trust and mutual understanding, leading to stronger and more meaningful relationships.
- **Enhanced Communication:** By actively listening and asking insightful questions, we become better communicators, able to express our thoughts and feelings clearly and effectively.
- **Increased Knowledge:** Every conversation is an opportunity to learn. Follow-up questions allow us to tap into the wisdom and experiences of others, expanding our knowledge and understanding of the world.
- **Improved Problem-Solving:** By exploring issues in depth and uncovering hidden perspectives, we can develop more creative and effective solutions to challenges.
- **Greater Innovation:** Deep conversations often spark new ideas and insights, leading to innovation in both personal and professional spheres.
- **Personal Growth:** By engaging in meaningful conversations, we gain a deeper understanding of ourselves, our values and our aspirations.

The art of follow-up questions is not a magic formula for instant success. It requires practice, patience and a genuine desire to connect with others. But with dedication and commitment, anyone can master this essential skill and unlock the transformative power of deep conversations.

Clarification and Elaboration

'The single biggest problem in communication is the illusion that it has taken place.'

—George Bernard Shaw

Misunderstandings are the potholes on the road to meaningful conversation. We've all experienced the frustration of misinterpreting someone's words or having our own twisted into something we didn't intend. The seemingly simple act of clarification and elaboration is the crucial bridge that spans these chasms of miscommunication, transforming shallow exchanges into profound dialogues.

The High Cost of Miscommunication

Consider the workplace, where a misinterpreted email can derail a project, or the dinner table, where an offhand comment can ignite a family feud. Miscommunication isn't just an inconvenience; it's a costly drain on our emotional energy and a barrier to building trust and connection. A study by the Holmes Report found that poor communication costs businesses an average of

$62.4 million per year.[*] But the financial cost is only the tip of the iceberg. The emotional toll of misunderstandings can lead to damaged relationships, missed opportunities and even physical and mental health problems.

The Power of Clarification

Clarification is the verbal equivalent of adjusting a microscope's focus. It brings fuzzy ideas into sharp relief, allowing us to truly understand what another person is trying to convey. A simple 'What do you mean by that?' or 'Could you elaborate on that point?' can open the door to deeper understanding and more meaningful conversation.

The Art of Elaboration

Elaboration, on the other hand, is the process of adding detail and nuance to our own ideas. It's the art of painting a vivid picture with words, allowing others to fully grasp our thoughts and feelings. When we elaborate, we move beyond vague generalities and into the realm of specific examples, personal anecdotes and vivid imagery.

---

[*] David Grossman, 'The Cost of Poor Communications, The Holmes Report. A survey of 400 companies with over 100,000 employees each'.

The Dance of Dialogue

Clarification and elaboration are not separate acts but rather two sides of the same coin. They are the yin and yang of meaningful conversation, the push and pull that propels us towards deeper understanding. When we ask for clarification, we invite the other person to elaborate. And when we elaborate, we create opportunities for others to seek clarification.

The Three 'C's of Clarification and Elaboration

- **Curiosity:** Approach conversations with a genuine desire to understand the other person's perspective. Let go of assumptions and judgements and embrace the unknown. Ask open-ended questions that invite elaboration and avoid leading questions that steer the conversation in a particular direction.
- **Courage:** Don't be afraid to ask for clarification, even if it feels awkward or uncomfortable. Remember, seeking clarification is not a sign of weakness but rather a demonstration of your commitment to understanding. And when it's your turn to elaborate, don't shy away from sharing your thoughts and feelings honestly and openly.
- **Compassion:** Listen with empathy and seek to understand the other person's emotional experience

as well as their intellectual perspective. Validate their feelings and acknowledge their pain points. When you elaborate, do so with sensitivity and respect, avoiding language that could be hurtful or offensive.

Beyond Words: Non-Verbal Cues

Clarification and elaboration are not limited to verbal communication. Our body language, facial expressions and tone of voice can also play a crucial role in conveying our understanding (or lack thereof). Paying attention to these non-verbal cues can help us gauge whether our message is being received as intended and adjust our communication accordingly.

The Ripple Effect of Clarification and Elaboration

The benefits of clarification and elaboration extend far beyond individual conversations. When we practise these skills regularly, we create a ripple effect that can transform our relationships, our workplaces and even our society as a whole. By fostering deeper understanding and more meaningful connections, we build a foundation for trust, cooperation and collaboration.

Embracing the Messiness of Communication

Communication is not a linear process but rather a messy, dynamic dance. There will be missteps, misunderstandings and moments of frustration. But by embracing the messiness and committing to the ongoing practice of clarification and elaboration, we can navigate these challenges with grace and emerge from each conversation with a deeper understanding of ourselves and others.

A Lifelong Journey, Not a Destination

The journey of deepening conversations through clarification and elaboration is not a one-time event but rather an ongoing practice. It requires patience, perseverance and a willingness to learn and grow. But the rewards are immeasurable. By honing these skills, we unlock the power of genuine connection, transforming our relationships and our lives in profound ways.

Encouraging Reflection

'The unexamined life is not worth living.'

—Socrates

This timeless quote by Socrates serves as a potent reminder that reflection isn't merely a philosophical exercise, but a vital component of a meaningful existence. In the context of deepening conversations, reflection acts as a wellspring, nourishing our interactions with depth and understanding. It allows us to delve beneath the surface of our exchanges, unearthing hidden nuances, assumptions and motivations.

Why Reflection Matters in Conversations

Conversations often become transactional, focused on conveying information or achieving specific outcomes. We may neglect the opportunity to pause, ponder and truly engage with the thoughts and feelings that arise during our interactions.

This is where reflection comes in, offering a counterbalance to the superficiality that can permeate our communication.

When we take the time to reflect, we:

- **Gain Self-Awareness:** We become more attuned to our own biases, emotions and triggers, which can influence how we participate in conversations.
- **Develop Empathy:** We step into the shoes of others, seeking to understand their perspectives, motivations and feelings.
- **Enhance Critical Thinking:** We analyse the information exchanged, questioning assumptions, identifying inconsistencies and seeking deeper truths.

- **Foster Creativity:** We generate new ideas, connections and possibilities that may not have emerged without thoughtful contemplation.
- **Strengthen Relationships:** We create a space for vulnerability, authenticity and trust, which are essential for building meaningful connections.

Cultivating a Reflective Mindset

Reflection isn't an innate skill; it's a practice that can be cultivated over time. Here are some strategies to incorporate reflection into your conversations:

- **Pause and Listen:** Resist the urge to jump in with your own thoughts immediately. Take a moment to truly absorb what the other person is saying, both verbally and non-verbally.
- **Ask Open-Ended Questions:** Encourage deeper exploration by asking questions that cannot be answered with a simple yes or no. Examples include:
  o 'What led you to that conclusion?'
  o 'How did that make you feel?'
  o 'What are the potential implications of this?'
- **Summarize and Clarify:** Restate what you've heard in your own words to ensure you've understood correctly. This also gives the other person an opportunity to elaborate or correct any misunderstandings.

- **Challenge Assumptions:** Gently question any assumptions you or the other person may be making. This can lead to new insights and perspectives.
- **Allow for Silence:** Don't feel pressured to fill every gap in the conversation. Silence can be a powerful tool for reflection, allowing thoughts and feelings to surface.
- **Journalling:** After a conversation, take some time to write down your reflections. This can help you process the experience, identify key takeaways and plan for future interactions.

The Transformative Power of Reflection

Reflection is a catalyst for transformation. It allows us to move beyond superficial exchanges and engage in dialogues that are meaningful, insightful and impactful.

By cultivating a reflective mindset, we open ourselves up to new possibilities, deeper connections and a greater understanding of ourselves and others.

Reflection as a Continuous Practice

Reflection is not a one-time event, but a continuous practice that can be integrated into all aspects of our lives. By making reflection a habit, we can enhance our communication skills, strengthen our relationships and live more fulfilling lives.

Incorporating Reflection into Group Conversations

In group settings, reflection can be even more powerful, as it allows multiple perspectives to be shared and explored. To encourage reflection in group conversations, consider these strategies:

- **Create a Safe Space:** Establish ground rules that encourage respect, openness and non-judgement.
- **Facilitate Discussion:** Guide the conversation with open-ended questions and prompts that encourage reflection.
- **Summarize Key Points:** Help the group synthesize their thoughts and identify common themes.
- **Encourage Individual Reflection:** Provide time for participants to reflect on their own before sharing with the group.

Reflection as a Gift

When we engage in reflection, we not only deepen our own understanding, but we also offer a gift to others. By demonstrating a willingness to listen, question and explore, we create a space where others feel safe to share their thoughts and feelings openly. This can lead to more authentic, meaningful and transformative conversations.

5

OVERCOMING BARRIERS TO EFFECTIVE QUESTIONING

Effective questioning is an essential skill for anyone who wants to be a successful communicator. However, some barriers can prevent us from asking effective questions. In this section, we will discuss these barriers and how to overcome them.

Common Mistakes and How to Avoid Them

> *'The important thing is not to stop questioning.*
> *Curiosity has its own reason for existence.'*
>
> —Albert Einstein

In the pursuit of knowledge and understanding, the art of asking the right questions is paramount. Yet, the path to effective questioning is fraught with potential pitfalls. In this chapter, we delve into common mistakes that hinder the effectiveness of questioning and explore strategies to sidestep these obstacles.

1. The Ambiguity Trap

One of the most prevalent mistakes is asking ambiguous questions. Vague or poorly defined questions can lead to confusion, misinterpretation and, ultimately, unsatisfactory answers. To avoid this trap, it is crucial to frame questions with clarity and precision.

- **Example:** Instead of asking, 'What do you think about the project?', consider asking, 'What specific aspects of the project's implementation do you believe could be improved?'
- **How to Avoid:** Before posing a question, take a moment to refine your wording. Ensure that the question is focused, specific and leaves no room for ambiguity.

2. The Leading Question Fallacy

Leading questions are designed to elicit a particular response, often confirming the questioner's preconceived notions. These questions can bias the answers received and hinder the exploration of alternative viewpoints.

- **Example:** Instead of asking, 'Don't you agree that this is the best course of action?', consider asking, 'What are your thoughts on the proposed course of action?'
- **How to Avoid:** Strive for neutrality in your questions. Avoid wording that suggests a preferred answer or implies a judgement of the respondent's perspective.

3. The Interrogation Pitfall

Bombarding someone with a barrage of questions can create an uncomfortable atmosphere akin to an interrogation. This approach can make the respondent feel defensive and less likely to provide thoughtful answers.

- **Example:** Instead of firing off multiple questions in rapid succession, consider asking one question at a time, allowing the respondent ample time to formulate a response.
- **How to Avoid**: Practise active listening and create a conversational flow. Pause between questions to allow for reflection and encourage a more natural exchange of information.

4. The Assumption Error

Making assumptions about the respondent's knowledge or opinions can lead to misunderstandings and missed opportunities for deeper exploration.

- **Example:** Instead of assuming that the respondent is familiar with a particular concept, consider asking, 'Could you please elaborate on your understanding of [concept]?'
- **How to Avoid:** Approach each question with an open mind and avoid making assumptions. Seek clarification when needed to ensure that both parties are on the same page.

5. The Closed-Ended Conundrum

While closed-ended questions (those with a limited range of possible answers) have their uses, overreliance on them can stifle meaningful dialogue.

- **Example:** Instead of asking, 'Are you satisfied with the outcome?', consider asking, 'What aspects of the outcome were most satisfying to you?'
- **How to Avoid:** Incorporate open-ended questions that invite elaboration and deeper exploration. These

questions encourage the respondent to share their thoughts and perspectives more fully.

6. The Confirmation Bias Culprit

Confirmation bias is the tendency to seek out information that confirms our existing beliefs and to discount information that contradicts them. This bias can influence the way we frame questions and interpret answers.

*   **Example:** Instead of seeking out information that supports your existing viewpoint, consider actively seeking out diverse perspectives and challenging your own assumptions.
*   **How to Avoid:** Be mindful of your own biases and strive for intellectual humility. Actively seek out information that challenges your preconceived notions.

7. The Lack of Follow-Up Flaw

Failing to ask follow-up questions can leave valuable insights unexplored. Follow-up questions can clarify ambiguities, delve deeper into a topic and uncover hidden nuances.

*   **Example:** Instead of simply accepting a surface-level answer, consider asking, 'Could you please elaborate

on that point?' or 'What factors contributed to that outcome?'

- **How to Avoid:** Cultivate a curiosity-driven mindset and be prepared to ask follow-up questions that probe deeper into the respondent's answers.

8. The 'Why' Question Quandary

While 'why' questions can be powerful tools for understanding motivations and reasoning, they can also be perceived as accusatory or judgemental.

- **Example:** Instead of asking, 'Why did you make that decision?', consider asking, 'What factors influenced your decision-making process?'
  How to Avoid: Use 'why' questions judiciously and consider alternative phrasing that focuses on understanding the underlying reasons behind a particular action or choice.

9. The Lack of Preparation Peril

Going into a conversation without adequate preparation can lead to aimless questioning and missed opportunities for meaningful dialogue.

- **Example:** Before engaging in a conversation, take the time to research the topic at hand, formulate relevant questions and anticipate potential areas of discussion.
- **How to Avoid:** Invest time in preparation to ensure that your questions are well-informed and targeted towards achieving your desired outcomes.

10. The Fear of Silence Folly

The discomfort of silence can sometimes lead us to fill the gaps with unnecessary questions or chatter. However, allowing for moments of silence can create space for reflection and deeper thought.

- **Example:** Instead of rushing to fill a silence, allow for a pause to give the respondent time to gather their thoughts and formulate a considered response.
- **How to Avoid:** Embrace the power of silence and recognize its value in facilitating meaningful conversation.

By being mindful of these common mistakes and implementing the suggested strategies, you can elevate your questioning skills and unlock a world of knowledge and understanding. Remember, effective questioning is not merely a means to an end; it is a journey of discovery, a quest for truth and a catalyst for growth.

Navigating Difficult Conversations

> *'The single biggest problem in communication is the illusion that it has taken place.'*
> —George Bernard Shaw

Misunderstandings, conflicts, disagreements . . . these are the thorns on the rosebush of human interaction. While we often yearn for smooth, harmonious dialogues, the reality is that difficult conversations are an inevitable part of life. Whether it's addressing a performance issue with a colleague, negotiating a contract with a client or resolving a personal dispute with a loved one, these interactions can be fraught with tension, anxiety and apprehension.

Yet, as Shaw's quote suggests, the most perilous conversations are often those where we believe we've communicated effectively, when in truth, the message has been lost, distorted or simply not received. This is where the art of overcoming barriers to effective questioning comes into play. It's about delving beneath the surface, probing for deeper understanding and fostering genuine dialogue even when the topics are sensitive, challenging or emotionally charged.

The High Cost of Avoidance

Consider the workplace. Studies have shown that the average employee spends 2.8 hours per week dealing with conflict. That's roughly 145 hours per year—nearly four full weeks of work—consumed by disagreements, misunderstandings and unresolved issues.

This not only takes a toll on individual productivity and well-being but also creates a toxic environment that can hinder collaboration, innovation and overall organizational performance.

The cost of avoidance extends far beyond the workplace. In personal relationships, the failure to address difficult conversations can lead to resentment, bitterness and, ultimately, the erosion of trust and intimacy. Whether it's a festering disagreement with a spouse, an unresolved conflict with a friend or a long-standing grudge against a family member, these unaddressed issues can create a rift that widens over time, ultimately leading to estrangement or even the dissolution of the relationship.

Unmasking the Barriers

Why do we shy away from difficult conversations? The reasons are as varied as the individuals involved, but some common barriers include:

- **Fear of Conflict:** Many of us are conflict-averse, preferring to sweep disagreements under the rug rather than risk confrontation. This can stem from a variety of factors, such as a desire to maintain harmony, a fear of rejection or a lack of confidence in our ability to handle conflict constructively.

- **Lack of Communication Skills:** Even when we're willing to engage in difficult conversations, we may lack the necessary skills to do so effectively. This can manifest as an inability to articulate our thoughts and feelings clearly, a tendency to become defensive or accusatory or difficulty listening actively and empathetically to the other person's perspective.

- **Emotional Baggage:** Past experiences, traumas or unresolved conflicts can create emotional baggage that makes it difficult to engage in present-day conversations. This can manifest as triggers, defensiveness or a tendency to project our own unresolved issues on to others.

- **Power Imbalances:** In situations where there's a significant power imbalance, such as between a boss and an employee or a parent and a child, the less powerful party may feel intimidated or silenced, making it difficult to speak up and address concerns.

The Power of Effective Questioning

Overcoming these barriers requires a multi-faceted approach, but one of the most powerful tools at our disposal is effective questioning. By asking the right questions, we can:

- **Uncover Hidden Assumptions and Biases:** Often, our disagreements stem from unspoken assumptions or unconscious biases that we haven't even acknowledged to ourselves. By asking probing questions, we can bring these hidden factors to the surface, allowing for a more honest and productive dialogue.
- **Clarify Misunderstandings:** Sometimes, the root of a conflict is simply a misunderstanding. By asking clarifying questions, we can ensure that we're on the same page and avoid talking past each other.
- **Explore Underlying Emotions:** Difficult conversations often involve strong emotions, such as anger, hurt or fear. By asking empathetic questions, we can create a safe space for the other person to express their emotions, leading to greater understanding and connection.
- **Generate New Insights and Solutions:** By asking open-ended questions, we can encourage creative thinking and problem-solving, leading to solutions that may not have been apparent at the outset.

The Art of Asking

Effective questioning is not about grilling the other person or trying to win an argument. It's about fostering genuine dialogue, building trust and working collaboratively towards a resolution. Some key principles to keep in mind include:

- **Ask with Curiosity, Not Judgement:** Approach the conversation with a genuine desire to understand the other person's perspective, rather than trying to prove them wrong or change their mind.
- **Listen Actively and Empathetically:** Pay attention not only to the words being spoken but also to the underlying emotions and non-verbal cues. Reflect on what you hear to ensure understanding and show that you're truly listening.
- **Avoid Leading Questions:** Leading questions are those that suggest a particular answer or bias the response. Instead, ask open-ended questions that allow for a range of responses.
- **Be Willing to Be Vulnerable:** Share your own thoughts, feelings and vulnerabilities. This can help to create a safe space for the other person to do the same.

Beyond the Conversation

While effective questioning is a crucial skill for navigating difficult conversations, it's important to remember that it's just one piece of the puzzle. Other factors, such as timing, environment and non-verbal communication, can also play a significant role in the outcome of the conversation.

Furthermore, it's important to recognize that not all difficult conversations will have a happy ending. Sometimes, despite our best efforts, we may be unable to reach a resolution or find common ground. In these cases, it's important to accept the limitations of the situation and move forward with grace and understanding.

The art of the uncomfortable is not about avoiding conflict or pretending that everything is fine. It's about embracing the challenges of human interaction, learning to communicate effectively even when the topics are difficult and building stronger, more resilient relationships in the process.

Handling Evasive Answers

'Ask the right questions if you're going to find the right answers.'

—Vanessa Redgrave

In communication, the art of asking effective questions is paramount. Yet, the path to uncovering the truth is not always straightforward. Evasive answers, like smokescreens, can obscure the information you seek, creating barriers to understanding. In this chapter, we delve into the realm of evasive answers, exploring their nature, motivations and, most importantly, strategies for navigating them.

The Elusive Nature of Evasive Answers

Evasive answers come in myriad forms, from vague generalizations to outright deflections. They may be cloaked in politeness, humour or even hostility. Recognizing evasive answers is the first step in overcoming them. Some common red flags include:

- **Non-Responsive Answers:** The response fails to address the question's core.
- **Vague Language:** The answer is filled with generalities, avoiding specifics.
- **Excessive Qualifiers:** The response is riddled with 'maybe', 'perhaps' or 'possibly'.
- **Deflection:** The answer shifts the focus away from the original question.
- **Attacking the Questioner:** The respondent becomes defensive or hostile.

The Motivations behind Evasion

Understanding why someone resorts to evasive answers is crucial in determining the best course of action.

Common motivations include:

- **Lack of Knowledge:** The person may not have the information you seek.
- **Protecting Sensitive Information:** The answer may involve confidential or embarrassing details.
- **Avoiding Conflict:** The respondent may fear disagreement or confrontation.
- **Manipulating the Conversation:** The person may be trying to control the narrative.

Strategies for Unmasking The Truth

Navigating evasive answers requires a combination of tact, persistence and effective questioning techniques. Consider the following strategies:

- **Clarify the Question:** Rephrase your question to ensure it is clear and specific. Avoid leading questions or loaded language that could trigger defensiveness.
- **Probe Deeper:** Ask follow-up questions that delve into the details. Use open-ended questions that encourage elaboration, rather than closed questions that can be answered with a simple 'yes' or 'no'.
- **Challenge Inconsistencies:** If you detect contradictions or inconsistencies in the responses, gently point them out and ask for clarification.

- **Appeal to Shared Interests:** If appropriate, try to frame your questions in a way that aligns with the respondent's goals or values.
- **Acknowledge Emotions:** If the person seems defensive or hesitant, acknowledge their feelings and assure them that you respect their position.
- **Be Patient and Persistent:** Don't give up easily. Sometimes, it takes multiple attempts and different approaches to elicit a genuine response.
- **Know When to Move On:** If the person continues to evade your questions, it may be time to change tactics or seek information from other sources.

Case Study: The Evasive Interviewee

Imagine you are a journalist interviewing a politician who is known for dodging questions. You ask a direct question about a controversial policy decision, and the politician responds with a vague statement about the importance of 'doing what's best for the country'. How do you handle this evasive answer?

First, you might clarify your question by asking, 'Can you be more specific about what you mean by "doing what's best for the country" in this particular context?'

If the politician continues to evade the question, you could probe deeper by asking, 'What are the potential benefits and drawbacks of this policy decision, in your opinion?'

If the politician still refuses to provide a direct answer, you might challenge their evasiveness by saying, 'Your response seems to avoid the specifics of my question. Can you address the concerns that have been raised about this policy?'

By employing these strategies, you increase the likelihood of getting a meaningful response, even from a notoriously evasive interviewee.

Advanced Techniques for Handling Evasive Answers

In some situations, more advanced techniques may be necessary to overcome evasive answers. These techniques include:

- **Reframing the Question:** Restate your question differently to elicit a different response.
- **Using Silence:** A well-timed pause can encourage the person to elaborate or fill the silence with additional information.
- **Employing Humour**: A light-hearted remark can diffuse tension and make the person more willing to open up.

The art of handling evasive answers is an ongoing process. By honing your questioning skills, understanding the motivations behind evasion and employing effective strategies, you can overcome communication barriers and uncover the truth. Remember, the most powerful questions are those that challenge assumptions, spark curiosity and, ultimately, lead to a deeper understanding of the world around us.

PART II

BUILDING CONFIDENCE

6

UNDERSTANDING CONFIDENCE

Confidence is a key factor in achieving success and self-fulfilment. It is the belief in oneself and one's abilities to accomplish a task or overcome a challenge. Having confidence can greatly impact our personal and professional lives, as it allows us to take risks, make decisions and handle difficult situations with ease.

But what exactly is confidence? And how do we develop it? Confidence comes from within. It is an inner state of mind that is shaped by our experiences, beliefs and attitudes. Some people are naturally confident, while others may struggle with low self-esteem. However, confidence is not a fixed trait—it can be developed and strengthened over time.

In this section, we will explore the concept of confidence in more detail and provide tips on how to cultivate and maintain it.

The Psychology of Confidence

'Our deepest fear is not that we are inadequate. Our deepest fear is that we are powerful beyond measure.'

—Marianne Williamson

Confidence, an intangible yet potent force, has captivated the human spirit for centuries. It is a quality that empowers individuals to embrace challenges, overcome obstacles and achieve their dreams. But what exactly is confidence? How does it manifest in our thoughts, emotions and behaviours? In this chapter, we embark on a journey to explore the intricate psychology of confidence, unravelling its complexities and shedding light on its transformative power.

The Multifaceted Nature of Confidence

Confidence is not a monolithic entity but rather a multifaceted construct with various dimensions. It encompasses beliefs about our abilities, feelings of self-efficacy and a sense of self-assuredness in social interactions. It is a dynamic state that fluctuates based on context, past experiences and personal values.

Confidence is a belief in our capacity to succeed. It is the conviction that we possess the skills, knowledge and resources necessary to achieve our goals. This belief is not based on blind optimism but rather on a realistic assessment of our strengths and weaknesses. Confident individuals acknowledge their limitations while maintaining a positive outlook on their overall capabilities.

Confidence also involves a feeling of self-efficacy or the belief that we can produce desired outcomes through our actions. This sense of agency empowers us to take initiative, persevere in the face of setbacks and, ultimately, achieve our objectives. It is the driving force behind our motivation and determination.

In social contexts, confidence manifests as a sense of self-assuredness and social efficacy. Confident individuals feel comfortable expressing their opinions, asserting their needs and navigating social interactions with ease. They are not afraid to speak up, take risks or put themselves out there.

The Roots of Confidence

Confidence is not an innate trait but rather a learnt behaviour.

It is shaped by our experiences, interactions with others and the messages we receive from our environment. Several factors contribute to the development of confidence:

- **Early Life Experiences:** Our early life experiences, particularly those involving parental support and encouragement, play a crucial role in shaping our self-esteem and confidence. Children who receive positive reinforcement for their efforts and accomplishments are more likely to develop a strong sense of self-efficacy and belief in their abilities.
- **Social Comparison:** Throughout our lives, we constantly compare ourselves to others. This social comparison process can either boost or diminish our confidence, depending on whether we perceive ourselves as superior or inferior to our peers.
- **Success and Failure:** Our past successes and failures also influence our confidence levels. Repeated successes reinforce our belief in our abilities, while repeated failures can erode our self-esteem and create a sense of learnt helplessness.
- **Social Support:** The support and encouragement we receive from others, particularly from significant figures such as parents, teachers and mentors, can significantly impact our confidence. Knowing that

others believe in us can bolster our own self-belief and motivate us to strive for greatness.

The Benefits of Confidence

Confidence is not merely a feel-good emotion; it has a profound impact on our lives. Confident individuals tend to:

- **Set and Achieve Ambitious Goals:** They are not afraid to dream big and pursue their passions with vigour.
- **Take Calculated Risks:** They are willing to step outside their comfort zones and embrace new challenges.
- **Persevere in the Face of Adversity:** They view setbacks as opportunities for growth and learning, rather than as reasons to give up.
- **Build Strong Relationships:** They are approachable, engaging and able to connect with others on a deeper level.
- **Lead and Inspire Others:** They are natural leaders, who can motivate and empower those around them.

In addition to these personal benefits, confidence also has a positive impact on our professional lives. Confident individuals are more likely to be seen as competent, credible and trustworthy. They are also more likely to be promoted, receive raises and negotiate better deals.

The Pitfalls of Overconfidence

While confidence is generally a positive trait, it is important to strike a balance. Overconfidence, or an inflated sense of one's abilities, can lead to poor decision-making, risk-taking behaviour and interpersonal conflict. Overconfident individuals may underestimate the challenges they face, overestimate their own abilities and ignore the advice of others.

It is also important to distinguish between confidence and arrogance. While confident individuals believe in their abilities, they are also humble and open to feedback. Arrogant individuals, on the other hand, have an inflated sense of self-importance and believe they are superior to others.

Cultivating Confidence

Confidence is not a fixed trait; it can be cultivated and strengthened over time. There are several strategies that individuals can use to boost their confidence:

- **Identify and Challenge Negative Self-Talk:** Negative self-talk, or the critical inner voice that tells us we are not good enough, can undermine our confidence. By recognizing and challenging these negative thoughts, we can replace them with more positive and empowering beliefs.

- **Focus on Your Strengths:** We all have unique talents and abilities. By focusing on our strengths, we can build a sense of self-efficacy and belief in our overall capabilities.

- **Set Realistic Goals:** Setting and achieving small, achievable goals can boost our confidence and motivate us to strive for bigger things.

- **Seek Out Challenges:** Stepping outside our comfort zones and embracing new challenges can help us expand our skills and knowledge, as well as build our confidence in our ability to adapt and overcome obstacles.

- **Surround Yourself with Positive People:** The people we spend time with can have a significant impact on our self-esteem and confidence. By surrounding ourselves with positive, supportive individuals, we can create a nurturing environment that fosters our growth and development.

Self-Esteem vs Confidence

'Confidence is not "Will they like me?". Confidence is "I'll be fine if they don't."'

—Christina Grimmie

This quote by Christina Grimmie, a singer tragically taken before her time, serves as a poignant introduction to the intricate dance between self-esteem and confidence. Often intertwined and used interchangeably, these two concepts are distinct entities that play a pivotal role in our personal and professional lives.

The Mirror: Self-Esteem

Self-esteem, often referred to as the mirror, is an internal reflection of our self-worth. It's the emotional evaluation we hold of our overall value as a person. This evaluation is influenced by various factors, including our experiences, relationships, achievements and societal standards.

A healthy level of self-esteem acts as a sturdy foundation, providing resilience in the face of adversity and empowering us to pursue our goals. However, when the mirror is distorted by negative self-talk, unrealistic expectations or societal pressures, our self-esteem can take a hit.

Think of self-esteem as a bank account. Positive experiences and affirmations act as deposits, bolstering our overall balance. Conversely, negative self-talk and setbacks act as withdrawals, depleting our emotional reserves. The challenge lies in maintaining a positive balance, ensuring that the deposits outweigh the withdrawals.

Research has shown a strong correlation between self-esteem and mental well-being. Individuals with high self-esteem tend to experience lower levels of stress, anxiety and depression. They are also more likely to exhibit resilience in the face of challenges, bounce back from setbacks and pursue their goals with greater determination. Conversely, low self-esteem can lead to a vicious cycle of self-doubt, fear of failure and social withdrawal.

The Compass: Confidence

Confidence, on the other hand, is the compass that guides our actions. It's the belief in our ability to succeed in a specific task or situation. Unlike self-esteem, which is an overall evaluation of our self-worth, confidence is more situational and task-specific. A person might have high self-esteem but lack confidence in public speaking. Similarly, someone with low self-esteem might possess unwavering confidence in their artistic abilities.

Confidence is not about being fearless or infallible. It's about acknowledging our fears and self-doubt yet choosing to move forward despite them. It's the internal voice that whispers, 'I can do this,' even when the odds seem stacked against us. This internal voice is built on a foundation of preparation, experience and a willingness to learn from our mistakes.

Studies have consistently demonstrated the positive impact of confidence on performance. When we believe in our abilities, we are more likely to take calculated risks, persevere in the face of obstacles and ultimately achieve our goals. Confidence can also enhance our social interactions, making us more approachable, persuasive and charismatic.

The Interplay: Where Self-Esteem and Confidence Meet

While self-esteem and confidence are distinct entities, they are not mutually exclusive. They often interact and influence each other. A healthy level of self-esteem can provide the bedrock upon which confidence is built. When we value ourselves and believe in our inherent worth, we are more likely to approach challenges with a confident mindset. Conversely, experiencing success in specific areas can bolster our overall self-esteem, creating a positive feedback loop.

However, it's important to note that self-esteem and confidence can also exist independently. A person might have high self-esteem but lack confidence in a particular skill or situation. Similarly, someone with low self-esteem might possess unwavering confidence in a specific area of expertise. This highlights the importance of recognizing the nuanced relationship between these two concepts.

The interplay between self-esteem and confidence can be likened to a dance. Self-esteem sets the stage, providing the emotional backdrop for our actions. Confidence, on the other hand, takes the lead, guiding our steps and propelling us towards our goals. When these two partners are in sync, the dance becomes effortless, graceful and empowering.

Nurturing Self-Esteem and Confidence

Developing healthy self-esteem and confidence is an ongoing journey, not a destination. It requires self-awareness, self-compassion and a willingness to step outside of our comfort zones. Here are some strategies to nurture both:

- **Challenge Negative Self-Talk:** Replace self-critical thoughts with positive affirmations.
- **Celebrate Your Achievements:** Acknowledge your successes, no matter how small they may seem.
- **Set Realistic Goals:** Break down large goals into smaller, achievable steps.
- **Learn from Your Mistakes:** View setbacks as opportunities for growth, not as personal failures.
- **Surround Yourself with Positive People:** Seek out supportive relationships that uplift and empower you.

- **Practise Self-Care:** Prioritize activities that nourish your mind, body and soul.

Remember, building self-esteem and confidence takes time and effort. Be patient with yourself, embrace the journey and celebrate every step forward.

7

DEVELOPING SELF-AWARENESS

Self-awareness is the ability to recognize and understand one's own emotions, thoughts and behaviours. It is a crucial skill for personal growth and development, as well as for building strong relationships with others. Developing self-awareness requires introspection, reflection and a willingness to confront uncomfortable truths about oneself.

Having self-awareness allows us to better understand our motivations, strengths, weaknesses and values. By being aware of these aspects of ourselves, we can make more informed decisions that align with our goals and values. It also helps us manage our emotions more effectively and develop healthy coping mechanisms for dealing with stress and difficult situations.

Self-awareness is essential for building strong relationships. When we are aware of our own emotions and behaviours, we can better understand how they may impact others. This allows us to communicate more effectively, show empathy and build trust with those around us.

Identifying Strengths and Weaknesses

'Our strengths and weaknesses are two sides of the same coin. One cannot exist without the other.'

—Anonymous

Every individual is a mosaic of traits, talents and tendencies. Some aspects of ourselves propel us forward, while others may hold us back. The journey of self-awareness is about recognizing and understanding these multifaceted dimensions—our strengths and weaknesses—and learning to leverage them for personal growth and fulfilment.

It's easy to be drawn to our strengths, the aspects of ourselves that come naturally and effortlessly. We may excel at communication, possess a sharp analytical mind, or have a natural ability to empathize with others. These are our shining attributes, talents and skills that make us unique and valuable.

However, it is equally important, if not more so, to acknowledge and understand our weaknesses. These are the areas where we struggle, the habits that hinder our progress or the fears that hold us back. While it might be tempting to ignore or downplay these aspects of ourselves, they are just as much a part of who we are as our strengths.

The Power of Strengths

Strengths are the driving forces behind our achievements and successes. They are the qualities that empower us to overcome challenges, pursue our goals and make a meaningful impact in our personal and professional lives.

Identifying and leveraging our strengths can lead to a multitude of benefits:

- **Increased Confidence:** Recognizing our strengths reinforces our belief in ourselves and our abilities, leading to greater self-assurance and a willingness to take on new challenges.
- **Improved Performance:** When we focus on our strengths, we are more likely to excel in our endeavours, as we are working in areas where we naturally thrive.
- **Enhanced Well-Being:** Utilizing our strengths can lead to a greater sense of satisfaction, purpose and overall happiness, as we are living in alignment with our true selves.

- **Greater Resilience:** Recognizing our strengths can help us bounce back from setbacks and adversity, as we know we have the inner resources to overcome obstacles.
- **Stronger Relationships:** By sharing our strengths with others, we can build deeper and more meaningful connections, as we reveal our authentic selves.

The Importance of Weaknesses

While strengths are essential, weaknesses are not to be overlooked or dismissed. Our weaknesses can be powerful catalysts for growth and self-improvement.

Understanding our weaknesses allows us to:

- **Identify Areas for Growth:** By acknowledging our weaknesses, we can pinpoint the areas where we need to develop and improve.
- **Set Realistic Goals:** When we are aware of our limitations, we can set achievable goals that are aligned with our true capabilities.
- **Seek Support:** Recognizing our weaknesses can encourage us to seek help and guidance from others, whether it be through mentorship, coaching or therapy.
- **Build Resilience:** By facing our weaknesses head-on, we can learn to overcome challenges and setbacks,

ultimately making us stronger and more resilient individuals.

- **Develop Humility:** Acknowledging our weaknesses can foster a sense of humility, as we recognize that we are not perfect and that we have room to grow.

The Dynamic Interplay

Strengths and weaknesses are not static or isolated entities. They are dynamic and interconnected, constantly influencing and shaping each other. What is a strength in one area can sometimes be a weakness in another. For example, a highly analytical person may also be prone to overthinking or analysis paralysis.

Furthermore, our strengths and weaknesses can evolve, depending on our experiences, personal growth and changing circumstances. What was once a weakness may become a strength through dedicated effort and development.

The Journey of Self-Discovery

Identifying and understanding our strengths and weaknesses is an ongoing process of self-discovery. It requires introspection, self-reflection and a willingness to confront both our positive and negative qualities.

Several tools and techniques can aid in this journey:

- **Self-Assessment:** Utilize personality tests, strengths assessments or 360-degree feedback tools to gain insights into your strengths and weaknesses.
- **Journalling:** Reflect on your experiences, successes and challenges, noting patterns and themes that emerge.
- **Seeking Feedback:** Ask trusted friends, family members or colleagues for their honest opinions and observations.
- **Professional Guidance:** Consider working with a therapist, coach or mentor who can provide objective feedback and support.

Remember, the goal is not to judge or criticize yourself, but rather to gain a deeper understanding of who you are and how you can best utilize your strengths and address your weaknesses for personal growth and fulfilment.

Embracing the Full Spectrum

Our strengths and weaknesses are not separate or opposing forces. They are two sides of the same coin, each equally important in shaping who we are and what we can achieve.

By embracing both our strengths and weaknesses, we can cultivate a holistic and balanced approach to personal development. We can leverage our strengths to achieve our goals, while simultaneously working on our weaknesses to overcome obstacles and reach our full potential.

In the words of the renowned psychologist Carl Jung, 'I would rather be whole than good.'

By acknowledging and accepting the full spectrum of our strengths and weaknesses, we can embark on a transformative journey of self-awareness, growth and fulfilment.

Mindfulness and Reflection

'The unexamined life is not worth living.'

—Socrates

The ancient Greek philosopher Socrates understood the fundamental importance of self-reflection. In our fast-paced, technology-driven world, it's easy to get swept away by the currents of daily life, neglecting the inner landscape of our thoughts, feelings and motivations. However, true self-awareness, a cornerstone of personal growth and development, requires us to slow down, turn inward and cultivate a mindful approach to our lives.

Mindfulness: More than Just a Buzzword

Mindfulness, often touted as a cure-all for modern ailments, is more than just a passing trend. It's a practice rooted in ancient traditions, adapted and refined for contemporary life. At its core, mindfulness involves paying full attention to the present moment without judgement. This might seem simple, but in our distraction-laden world, it can be surprisingly challenging.

Research has shown that practising mindfulness can yield a wide range of benefits, including:

- **Reduced Stress and Anxiety:** Mindfulness helps us become aware of our stress triggers and develop healthier coping mechanisms.
- **Improved Focus and Concentration:** By training our minds to stay present, we enhance our ability to concentrate on tasks and avoid mental clutter.
- **Increased Self-Awareness:** Mindfulness allows us to observe our thoughts and feelings without getting caught up in them, leading to a greater understanding of ourselves.
- **Enhanced Emotional Regulation:** By recognizing our emotions as they arise, we can respond to them more skilfully and avoid impulsive reactions.
- **Stronger Relationships:** Mindfulness cultivates empathy and compassion, essential ingredients for healthy connections with others.

Reflection: Turning Inward for Growth

While mindfulness anchors us in the present, reflection invites us to delve into the past and contemplate the future. It's a process of examining our experiences, actions and choices to gain deeper insights into ourselves. Reflection can take many forms:

- **Journalling:** Writing down our thoughts and feelings can help us clarify our emotions and identify patterns in our behaviour.
- **Meditation:** Reflective meditation involves focusing on a specific question or theme to gain clarity and understanding.
- **Conversations with Trusted Friends or Mentors:** Sharing our experiences with others can provide valuable perspectives and feedback.

Through reflection, we can:

- **Learn from Our Mistakes:** By examining our past errors, we can avoid repeating them and make wiser choices in the future.
- **Identify Our Values and Priorities:** Reflecting on our actions helps us understand what truly matters to us.
- **Set Meaningful Goals:** By considering our aspirations and dreams, we can chart a course towards a more fulfilling life.

- **Cultivate Gratitude:** Reflecting on our blessings helps us appreciate the good in our lives and fosters a positive outlook.

The Synergy of Mindfulness and Reflection

Mindfulness and reflection are not mutually exclusive practices; they complement each other in powerful ways. Mindfulness lays the groundwork for self-awareness by enabling us to observe our thoughts and feelings without judgement. This non-reactive awareness provides the raw material for reflection, allowing us to examine our experiences with greater clarity and objectivity.

Conversely, reflection deepens our mindfulness practice by giving us insights into our habitual patterns of thinking and behaviour. These insights enable us to make more conscious choices in the present moment, aligning our actions with our values and goals.

Cultivating a Mindful and Reflective Life

Integrating mindfulness and reflection into our daily lives doesn't require a complete overhaul of our routines. Even small changes can yield significant results. Here are a few tips to get started:

- **Start a Mindfulness Practice:** Set aside a few minutes each day to simply sit and focus on your breath. Observe your thoughts and feelings without judgement.

- **Keep a Journal:** Write down your thoughts, feelings and experiences regularly. Use your journal as a space for self-exploration and reflection.
- **Schedule Regular Reflection Time:** Set aside time each week to reflect on your experiences and goals. This could be a dedicated meditation session, a walk in nature or a conversation with a trusted friend.
- **Be Curious and Open-Minded:** Approach your inner world with a sense of curiosity and openness. Allow yourself to be surprised by what you discover.
- **Practise Self-Compassion:** Be kind and understanding towards yourself as you explore your inner landscape. Remember, everyone makes mistakes and has room for growth.

The Journey of Self-Discovery

Developing self-awareness is not a destination but a lifelong journey. As we cultivate mindfulness and reflection, we embark on a path of self-discovery, uncovering hidden strengths, confronting challenging emotions and, ultimately, living a more authentic and fulfilling life.

8

PRACTICAL STRATEGIES FOR BUILDING CONFIDENCE

Confidence is a quality that can assist us in confronting the challenges that we encounter in life. An overwhelming majority of us are familiar with the sensation of carrying out a task with self-assurance, while at the same time, it is a frequent experience to have a lack of confidence. On the other hand, how can we increase our self-assurance? In this section, we will explore some practical strategies that can help you build and maintain your confidence.

Setting and Achieving Goals

'The only limit to our realization of tomorrow will be our doubts of today.'

—Franklin D. Roosevelt

This quote, as simple as it may seem, holds profound wisdom when it comes to the topic of setting and achieving goals. Our doubts can indeed become roadblocks on our path to success. But by overcoming these doubts and taking decisive action, we open ourselves up to a world of possibilities.

It's a fundamental truth that goals propel us forward. They give us direction, a sense of purpose and a reason to wake up each morning. When we set goals and work towards achieving them, we gain a sense of control over our lives, a feeling that we are actively shaping our destinies.

The Power of Goal-Setting

Setting goals is a powerful tool for personal development and growth. It's a skill that can be learnt and honed over time. Think of it as a muscle that gets stronger with regular exercise. By regularly setting and achieving goals, we build resilience, self-efficacy and a belief in our own abilities.

Goals act as a compass, guiding us through the complexities of life. They help us prioritize our efforts, make better decisions and avoid distractions. Goals can be big or small, short-term or long-term, personal or professional. The most important thing is that they are meaningful to you and aligned with your values and aspirations.

Goals also give us a sense of accomplishment and fulfilment. When we achieve a goal, we experience a surge of dopamine, a neurotransmitter that plays a key role in motivation and reward. This positive reinforcement strengthens our neural pathways, making it easier to set and achieve future goals.

The Importance of Confidence in Goal Achievement

Confidence is a critical ingredient in the recipe for success. When we believe in ourselves and our abilities, we are more likely to take on challenges, persevere in the face of setbacks and, ultimately, achieve our goals. Confidence is not about arrogance or overestimating our abilities. It's about having a realistic assessment of our strengths and weaknesses and a belief that we have what it takes to succeed.

Confidence is often the difference between those who succeed and those who fall short. When faced with obstacles, those with high levels of confidence are more likely to see them as opportunities for growth rather than reasons to give up. They are more willing to take calculated risks, step outside their comfort zones and embrace the unknown.

Confidence can be cultivated through various means, such as positive self-talk, visualization and surrounding yourself with supportive people. It's also important to celebrate your successes, no matter how small they may seem. Each achievement, whether it's completing a project at work or overcoming a personal challenge, reinforces your belief in your own abilities.

Practical Strategies for Setting and Achieving Goals

- **Define Your Goals:** The first step is to identify what you want to achieve. Be specific and clear about your goals. Instead of saying, 'I want to be healthier,' say, 'I want to lose ten pounds in three months by exercising regularly and eating a balanced diet.'
- **Set SMART Goals:** Make sure your goals are Specific, Measurable, Achievable, Relevant and Time-Bound. This will make them more tangible and actionable.
- **Create a Plan:** Break down your goals into smaller, more manageable steps. This will make them less overwhelming and more achievable.
- **Take Action:** The most important step is to start working towards your goals. Don't wait for the perfect moment or for all the conditions to be right. Take the first step, and then the next, and the next.
- **Track Your Progress:** Regularly review your progress and make adjustments as needed. Celebrate your successes and learn from your setbacks.
- **Stay Motivated:** Motivation can fluctuate, so it's important to find ways to keep yourself inspired. This could involve reminding yourself of your reasons for

setting the goal, visualizing yourself achieving it or surrounding yourself with supportive people.

- **Don't Give Up:** There will be obstacles and setbacks along the way. Don't let them discourage you. Learn from your mistakes, adjust your approach and keep moving forward. Remember, persistence is key to achieving any goal.

Overcoming Obstacles to Goal Achievement

The journey towards goal achievement is rarely a smooth one. Obstacles and challenges are inevitable. However, it's how we respond to these challenges that determine our success. Those who possess resilience and a strong sense of self-belief are more likely to overcome obstacles and stay on track towards their goals.

One common obstacle is fear. Fear of failure, fear of the unknown and fear of not being good enough can hold us back from taking action and pursuing our dreams. To overcome fear, it's important to recognize that it's a natural human emotion. Everyone experiences fear at some point in their lives. The key is to not let fear paralyse you. Instead, use it as fuel to propel you forward. Reframe fear as excitement and embrace the challenges that come your way.

Another obstacle is procrastination. Procrastination is the act of delaying or postponing a task or set of tasks. It's a common problem that can stem from various factors, such as fear of failure, perfectionism or feeling overwhelmed. To overcome procrastination, it's helpful to break down tasks into smaller, more manageable chunks, set deadlines and reward yourself for completing each step. It's also important to identify your triggers for procrastination and find strategies to manage them.

Distractions are another obstacle that can derail our efforts towards goal achievement. In today's digital age, distractions are everywhere. Social media, emails, notifications and the constant barrage of information can easily pull us away from our goals. To minimize distractions, it's helpful to create a dedicated workspace, turn off notifications and set boundaries on your technology use. It's also important to prioritize your tasks and focus on one thing at a time.

Lack of support can also be a barrier to goal achievement. It's important to surround yourself with people who believe in you and your goals. Having a support system can provide encouragement, motivation and accountability. If you don't have a strong support system in your immediate circle, consider joining a group or finding a mentor, who can offer guidance and support.

The Role of Mindset in Goal Achievement

Our mindset plays a significant role in our ability to set and achieve goals. A growth mindset, as opposed to a fixed mindset, is essential for success. People with a growth mindset believe that their abilities can be developed through dedication and hard work. They embrace challenges, persist in the face of setbacks and see effort as a path to mastery.

On the other hand, people with a fixed mindset believe that their abilities are static and cannot be changed. They avoid challenges, give up easily and see effort as fruitless or worse, a sign of weakness. This mindset can be limiting and prevent individuals from reaching their full potential.

Cultivating a growth mindset involves challenging negative self-talk, reframing setbacks as learning opportunities and focusing on effort rather than innate ability. It's also important to celebrate small wins, learn from mistakes and surround yourself with people who encourage and support your growth.

Remember, achieving goals is not just about reaching the finish line. It's about the journey, the growth and the lessons learnt along the way. By setting goals, building confidence and adopting a growth mindset, we empower ourselves to create the lives we desire and leave a lasting impact on the world.

Positive Self-Talk and Affirmations

*'Whether you think you can, or you think you can't—
you're right.'*

—Henry Ford

Ford's quote, though simple, is a profound reflection of the power of our inner dialogue. Consider this: research shows that the average person has about 60,000 thoughts a day. That's an incredible amount of mental chatter! Now, imagine if the majority of those thoughts were negative, self-doubting or fear-based. What kind of impact would that have on your confidence and ability to take action?

Conversely, what if a large portion of those thoughts were positive, encouraging and empowering? This is where the transformative practice of positive self-talk and affirmations comes into play.

Understanding Positive Self-Talk

Positive self-talk is exactly what it sounds like: the practice of speaking kindly and encouragingly to yourself. It's about noticing and challenging negative thought patterns and replacing them with more constructive and optimistic ones. It's the inner voice that says, 'You've got this!' instead of, 'You're going to fail.'

Positive self-talk isn't about denying challenges or difficulties. It's about approaching those challenges with a positive mindset and believing in your ability to learn, grow and overcome obstacles. It's about cultivating a sense of self-compassion and understanding, recognizing that everyone makes mistakes and that setbacks are a natural part of the learning process.

The Science Behind Affirmations

Affirmations are short, positive statements that you repeat to yourself regularly. They are designed to re-programme your subconscious mind, helping you to believe in the positive statements you're affirming. While it might seem too good to be true, there's actually a growing body of scientific evidence supporting the effectiveness of affirmations.

Neuroscience research has shown that repeating affirmations can activate the reward centres in your brain, releasing feel-good chemicals like dopamine. This can help boost your mood, motivation and overall sense of well-being. Additionally, affirmations can help strengthen neural pathways associated with positive emotions and beliefs, making it easier to think and feel positive over time.

Creating Effective Affirmations

Not all affirmations are created equal. To be truly effective, affirmations should be:

- **Personal:** Tailor your affirmations to your specific goals and challenges. What do you want to believe about yourself? What limiting beliefs are you trying to overcome?

- **Positive:** Frame your affirmations in a positive light. Avoid using negative words like 'don't' or 'can't'.
- **Present Tense:** Write your affirmations as if they are already true. This helps to reinforce the belief that what you're affirming is possible.
- **Specific:** Be clear and concise in your affirmations. Avoid vague or general statements.
- **Emotional:** Infuse your affirmations with emotion. How do you want to feel? Use words that evoke those emotions.

Examples of Powerful Affirmations

Here are a few examples of powerful affirmations you can use:

- 'I am confident and capable.'
- 'I am worthy of love and respect.'
- 'I am strong and resilient.'
- 'I am attracting abundance into my life.'
- 'I am grateful for all that I have.'

Incorporating Affirmations into Your Daily Routine

The key to making affirmations work is consistency. Make a habit of repeating your affirmations several times a day. You can say them out loud, write them down or even create visual reminders. Find what works best for you and stick with it.

Here are a few ideas for incorporating affirmations into your daily routine:

- Say them while looking in the mirror.
- Write them down in a journal.
- Create affirmation cards and place them around your home or office.
- Repeat them silently throughout the day.
- Listen to audio recordings of your affirmations.
- Use a mobile app to remind you to repeat your affirmations.

The Power of Combining Positive Self-Talk and Affirmations

When you combine positive self-talk with affirmations, you create a powerful synergy that can accelerate your personal growth and transformation. Positive self-talk helps you catch and challenge negative thoughts in the moment, while affirmations work to re-programme your subconscious mind over time.

Together, these practices can help you:

- Increase your self-confidence
- Improve your self-esteem

- Reduce stress and anxiety
- Enhance your motivation and focus
- Achieve your goals
- Live a more fulfilling and joyful life

Building confidence is a journey, not a destination. It takes time, effort and commitment. But with the right tools and strategies, you can cultivate the inner strength and resilience you need to overcome any challenge and create the life you desire. Positive self-talk and affirmations are two of the most powerful tools you have at your disposal.

Embracing Failure and Learning from It

> *'Ever tried. Ever failed. No matter. Try again. Fail again. Fail better.'*
>
> —Samuel Beckett

Beckett's words, though stark, hold a profound truth. Failure isn't a full stop; it's a comma, a pause before the next sentence begins. In our pursuit of confidence, we often view failure as an adversary, a setback to be avoided at all costs. Yet, paradoxically, it is in our failures that we often find the most potent catalysts for growth and transformation.

A New Perspective on Failure

Imagine this: a toddler learning to walk. They stumble, they fall, they cry. But do they give up? No. They get back up, again and again, each time adjusting their approach, refining their balance until one day they take those first wobbly steps. We celebrate those steps, not the falls. Why then, as adults, do we treat our own stumbles with such disdain?

Consider these statistics:

- Seventy per cent of successful entrepreneurs have experienced at least one major business failure.
- Michael Jordan, widely regarded as one of the greatest basketball players of all time, missed over 9000 shots in his career.
- J.K. Rowling's *Harry Potter* manuscript was rejected by twelve different publishers before finding a home.

These are not stories of defeat; they are stories of resilience, determination and the extraordinary power of learning from failure.

The Anatomy of Failure

Failure is not a monolithic entity. It comes in many forms, from minor setbacks to catastrophic collapses. Each type of failure offers unique lessons if we are willing to look for them.

- **Failures of Knowledge:** These occur when we lack the information or skills needed for a task. The lesson here is to seek out the knowledge we lack, to learn and grow.
- **Failures of Strategy:** These arise when our plans are flawed or poorly executed. The lesson is to analyse what went wrong, refine our strategies and try again.
- **Failures of Environment:** Sometimes, external factors beyond our control contribute to our failure. The lesson is to adapt to changing circumstances and to be flexible and resourceful.

Regardless of the type of failure, the key is to shift our mindset from one of self-blame and shame to one of curiosity and learning.

The Learning Process

So, how do we transform failure from a roadblock to a stepping stone? Here are some practical strategies:

1. **Acknowledge and Accept:** The first step is to acknowledge the failure and to own it without

judgement. This is not about wallowing in self-pity; it's about creating space for honest reflection.

2. **Analyse and Understand:** Once you've accepted the failure, it's time to analyse it. What went wrong? What were the contributing factors? What could you have done differently?

3. **Extract the Lessons**: Every failure, no matter how small, holds valuable lessons. What did you learn about yourself, your abilities and your approach? These lessons are the seeds of future growth.

4. **Apply and Adapt:** Don't just learn from your mistakes; apply those lessons to your future endeavours. Adjust your strategies, refine your approach and try again with renewed vigour.

The Confidence Connection

Embracing failure and learning from it has a profound impact on our confidence. When we overcome setbacks and emerge stronger, our belief in ourselves grows. We realize that failure is not a reflection of our worth, but an opportunity for growth.

Moreover, as we become more comfortable with failure, we are more willing to take risks, step outside our comfort zones and pursue our dreams with boldness and courage. This, in turn, fuels our confidence and propels us towards our goals.

The Gift of Failure

Failure is not something to be feared, but a gift to be unwrapped. It is in our failures that we discover our resilience, our determination and our capacity for growth. By embracing failure and learning from it, we not only build our confidence but also unlock our full potential.

9

CONFIDENCE IN ACTION

When you have a high level of confidence, it shows in your actions. It gives you the courage to take risks and try new things without fear of failure. This can be especially beneficial in a professional setting where confidence is often key to success.

In this section, we will discuss the importance of confidence in action and how to cultivate it in our daily lives.

Body Language and Non-Verbal Cues

'The most important thing in communication is hearing what isn't said.'

—Peter Drucker

Have you ever walked into a room and instantly felt the energy shift? Perhaps a charismatic speaker took the stage, or a powerful leader entered the boardroom. Their words might have been captivating, but it's often their unspoken language that leaves a lasting impression. The way they hold themselves, the subtle gestures, the intensity of their gaze—these are the non-verbal cues that speak volumes about their confidence and influence.

The Unspoken Language of Power

Body language, the silent symphony of communication, plays a pivotal role in how we perceive and interact with others. It's a complex dance of postures, gestures, facial expressions and even micro-movements that reveal our innermost thoughts and feelings. While our words may convey information, our bodies broadcast our true intentions, emotions and level of confidence.

Consider a job interview scenario. Two candidates with identical qualifications walk through the door. One sits hunched over, avoiding eye contact and fidgeting nervously. The other stands tall, offers a firm handshake and maintains a steady gaze. Who do you think exudes more confidence and is more likely to get the job?

Research suggests that non-verbal cues account for a staggering 55 per cent of our communication, while words make up only 7 per cent. The remaining 38 per cent is attributed to tone of voice. This means that even the most eloquent speech can fall flat if not accompanied by congruent body language.

The Confidence Code: Mastering Non-Verbal Cues

Confidence, like any skill, can be honed and refined. And a significant part of cultivating confidence lies in mastering the art of non-verbal communication. Here are some key non-verbal cues that convey confidence and influence:

- **Posture:** Stand tall with your shoulders back and your head held high. This open posture signals confidence and approachability. Avoid slouching or crossing your arms, as these can appear defensive or closed off.
- **Eye Contact:** Maintain steady eye contact when speaking and listening. This demonstrates attentiveness and sincerity. However, avoid staring, as it can be perceived as aggressive.
- **Facial Expressions:** A genuine smile is a universal symbol of warmth and confidence. It puts others at ease and makes you appear more approachable. Practise smiling even when you don't feel like it—it can actually boost your mood.
- **Hand Gestures:** Use open and expansive hand gestures to emphasize your points and convey

enthusiasm. Avoid fidgeting or hiding your hands, as this can betray nervousness.

- **Voice:** Speak clearly and confidently, projecting your voice without shouting. Vary your tone and pace to keep your audience engaged. Avoid fillers like 'um' or 'ah', as they can undermine your credibility.
- **Personal Space:** Respect others' personal space but don't be afraid to claim your own. Standing too close can be intrusive while standing too far away can seem aloof.

Confidence in Action: Applying Non-Verbal Cues

Mastering non-verbal cues is not about putting on a facade of confidence. It's about aligning your inner state with your outer expression. When you feel confident on the inside, it naturally shines through in your body language. And when you consciously adopt confident body language, it can actually boost your inner confidence.

Practise these non-verbal cues in your everyday interactions. Notice how others respond to you. Experiment with different postures, gestures and facial expressions. Over time, you'll develop a repertoire of non-verbal behaviours that project confidence and influence in any situation.

Assertiveness vs Aggressiveness

'The difference between being assertive and being aggressive is how our words and behaviour affect the rights and well-being of others.'

—Sharon Anthony Bower

In confident communication, assertiveness is often lauded as the gold standard. It allows us to express our needs, opinions and boundaries clearly and directly while respecting the rights of others. However, there's a fine line between assertiveness and its less desirable counterpart, aggressiveness.

This chapter will delve into the nuances of both communication styles, exploring how to harness the power of assertiveness while avoiding the pitfalls of aggressiveness.

Understanding Assertiveness

Assertiveness, in essence, is the ability to stand up for oneself and communicate one's needs and desires respectfully and confidently. It involves advocating for oneself while also valuing the perspectives of others. Assertive individuals express their thoughts and feelings openly and honestly, but they do so without infringing upon the rights or feelings of others.

Key Characteristics of Assertiveness

- **Direct and Honest Communication:** Assertive individuals communicate directly and honestly, expressing their thoughts, feelings and needs clearly and without ambiguity.
- **Respect for Others:** Assertiveness involves respecting the opinions, feelings and rights of others, even when disagreeing with them.
- **Active Listening:** Assertive communicators are active listeners, paying attention to what others are saying and responding thoughtfully.
- **Calm and Confident Demeanour:** Assertiveness is characterized by a calm and confident demeanour, even in challenging situations.
- **Ability to Say No:** Assertive individuals are comfortable saying 'no' when necessary, without feeling guilty or obligated.
- **Use of 'I' Statements:** Assertive communicators use 'I' statements to express their feelings and needs, taking ownership of their emotions.

Benefits of Assertiveness

Assertiveness offers a multitude of benefits for both personal and professional life.

These include:

- **Improved Relationships:** Assertiveness fosters healthier relationships by promoting open communication and mutual respect.
- **Reduced Stress and Anxiety:** Assertive individuals experience less stress and anxiety because they can express their needs and concerns.
- **Increased Self-Esteem:** Assertiveness builds self-esteem by empowering individuals to advocate for themselves.
- **Enhanced Problem-Solving:** Assertive communication can lead to more effective problem-solving by encouraging collaboration and understanding.
- **Greater Influence:** Assertive individuals are often more influential because they can clearly articulate their ideas and persuade others.

The Dark Side of Aggressiveness

Aggressiveness, on the other hand, is a communication style characterized by hostility, disrespect and a disregard for the feelings and rights of others. Aggressive individuals often resort to intimidation, manipulation or verbal attacks to get their way.

Key Characteristics of Aggressiveness

- **Hostile and Disrespectful Communication:** Aggressive individuals often use harsh language, insults and personal attacks when communicating.
- **Dominating Behaviour:** Aggressiveness involves trying to control or dominate others, often through intimidation or manipulation.
- **Lack of Empathy:** Aggressive communicators show little or no empathy for the feelings of others.
- **Blaming and Accusing:** Aggressive individuals tend to blame others for their problems and accuse them of wrongdoing.
- **Threats and Ultimatums:** Aggressive communicators may use threats or ultimatums to get what they want.
- **Escalation of Conflict:** Aggressiveness often leads to escalation of conflict, making it difficult to find solutions or compromise.

Consequences of Aggressiveness

Aggressiveness can have severe negative consequences:

- **Damaged Relationships:** Aggressiveness can damage relationships, leading to resentment, anger and distrust.

- **Increased Stress and Conflict:** Aggressive communication can create a hostile environment, leading to increased stress and conflict.
- **Isolation:** Aggressive individuals may find themselves isolated as others avoid their confrontational behaviour.
- **Loss of Respect:** Aggressiveness can erode respect from others, making it difficult to build trust or influence.
- **Negative Health Effects:** Chronic aggressiveness has been linked to negative health effects, such as high blood pressure and heart disease.

Striking the Balance: Assertiveness in Action

The key to confident communication lies in striking the balance between assertiveness and respect. It's about advocating for oneself while also valuing the perspectives of others. Here are some strategies for practising assertiveness in your daily life:

- **Know Your Rights:** Understand your rights and boundaries and be willing to defend them respectfully.
- **Use 'I' Statements:** Express your feelings and needs using 'I' statements, rather than blaming or accusing others.
- **Be Direct and Honest:** Communicate your thoughts and feelings directly and honestly, without being passive or aggressive.

- **Practise Active Listening:** Pay attention to what others are saying; respond thoughtfully and respectfully.
- **Be Calm and Confident:** Maintain a calm and confident demeanour, even in challenging situations.
- **Learn to Say 'No':** Don't be afraid to say 'no' when necessary, without feeling guilty or obligated.
- **Seek Win-Win Solutions:** Aim for solutions that benefit both you and the other person involved.
- **Manage Your Emotions:** Learn to manage your emotions, especially anger and frustration.
- **Practise, Practise, Practise:** Assertiveness is a skill that takes practice. The more you use it, the more natural it will become.

Remember: Assertiveness is not about being perfect. It's about being willing to speak up for yourself and express your needs respectfully and confidently.

Speaking Up in Groups

> 'The only way to do great work is to love what you do. If you haven't found it yet, keep looking. Don't settle.'
>
> —Steve Jobs

Have you ever sat in a meeting with an idea burning in your mind, but fear held you back from sharing it? Or perhaps you voiced your opinion, only to have it dismissed or overshadowed? You're not alone. Some people experience a certain level of anxiety when speaking in groups. This is a phenomenon known as glossophobia or the fear of public speaking. But what if I told you this fear is not a life sentence? What if the key to unlocking your confidence and making your voice heard lies in action?

Confidence, like any muscle, needs to be exercised. It's not about eradicating fear but learning to dance with it. This chapter will guide you through practical strategies and actionable steps to speak up in groups, turning your fear into fuel for your voice.

Understanding the Fear

Fear is a primal instinct, designed to protect us from danger. However, in the modern world, the dangers we face are often not life-threatening but social. The fear of judgement, rejection or ridicule can paralyse us, preventing us from taking the risks necessary for growth.

But here's the secret: everyone feels fear. Even the most seasoned speakers experience butterflies before taking the stage. The difference is that confident speakers have learnt to channel their fear into excitement and anticipation. They see fear as a sign that they're about to step outside their comfort zone and into a realm of growth and possibility.

The Power of Preparation

One of the most effective ways to combat fear is through preparation. This doesn't mean memorizing a script (in fact, that can often make you sound robotic and inauthentic), but rather, it involves thoroughly understanding your topic, anticipating potential questions and practising your delivery.

Start by researching your topic inside and out. The more knowledgeable you are, the more confident you'll feel. Then, consider the different perspectives and questions that might arise. This will help you think on your feet and respond effectively.

Practise is key. Rehearse your presentation in front of a mirror, record yourself or practise with a friend or family member. The more you practise, the more comfortable and confident you'll become.

Finding Your Voice

Your voice is unique, and it deserves to be heard. But sometimes, we need to dig a little deeper to discover its full potential. Here are a few tips:

- **Identify Your Values:** What are the things that matter most to you? What are you passionate about? When you speak from your values, your voice will naturally carry more weight and conviction.

- **Know Your Audience:** Who are you speaking to? What are their interests and concerns? Tailor your message to resonate with your audience, and you'll be more likely to capture their attention and respect.
- **Embrace Your Authentic Self:** Don't try to be someone you're not. Let your personality shine through in your words and delivery. People are drawn to authenticity, and it will make you a more engaging and memorable speaker.

Speaking Up with Confidence

Now that you've prepared and found your voice, it's time to speak up. Here are some strategies to help you project confidence and make an impact:

- **Start Strong:** Your opening sets the tone for your entire presentation. Begin with a powerful statement, a thought-provoking question or a captivating story to grab your audience's attention.
- **Use Your Body Language:** Non-verbal communication is just as important as your words. Stand tall, make eye contact and use gestures to emphasize your points. Your body language should convey confidence and enthusiasm.
- **Speak Clearly and Concisely:** Avoid filler words like 'um' and 'ah'. Speak at a moderate pace, enunciate

your words and use pauses for emphasis. Your voice should be clear, strong and easy to understand.

- **Connect with Your Audience:** Engage your audience by asking questions, inviting participation or sharing personal anecdotes. Make eye contact with different people in the room to create a sense of connection.

Overcoming Obstacles

Speaking up in groups is not without its challenges. You might encounter interruptions, disagreements or even hostility. But these obstacles are not roadblocks—they're growth opportunities.

If you're interrupted, politely acknowledge the interruption and then continue with your point. If you face disagreement, listen respectfully to the other person's perspective and then calmly present your own. If you encounter hostility, remain calm and professional and don't take it personally. Remember, you have the right to be heard, and your voice matters.

The Ripple Effect of Speaking Up

Speaking up in groups is not just about personal gain; it's about creating a ripple effect of positive change. When you share your ideas, you inspire others to do the same. You spark new conversations, challenge the status quo and contribute to a more inclusive and dynamic environment.

Your voice is a powerful tool for change. It can ignite movements, inspire action and transform the world around you. So don't let fear hold you back. Step up, speak up and let your voice be heard.

Remember: Confidence is not the absence of fear but the triumph over it. The more you speak up, the more confident you'll become. And the more confident you become, the more impact you'll make. So go out there and make your voice count. The world is waiting to hear what you have to say.

Additional Tips

- **Join a Toastmasters Club:** Toastmasters International is a non-profit educational organization that teaches public speaking and leadership skills through a worldwide network of clubs.
- **Take a Public Speaking Course:** Many online and offline courses can help you improve your public speaking skills.
- **Read Books and Articles on Public Speaking:** There are many resources available to help you learn more about public speaking and overcome your fear.
- **Seek Feedback:** Ask friends, family or colleagues for feedback on your presentations. This can help you identify areas where you can improve.

Speaking up in groups is a skill that takes time and practice to develop. But with the right strategies and a willingness to step outside your comfort zone, you can become a confident and influential speaker.

10

COPING WITH CRITICISM

'The trouble with most of us is that we would rather
be ruined by praise than saved by criticism.'

—Norman Vincent Peale

The world isn't always a gentle place. Whether it's a disapproving look from a parent, a scathing performance review or a social media pile-on, criticism can sting. In a society that often equates success with constant approval, facing disapproval can feel like a personal attack, chipping away at our confidence and leaving us questioning our abilities. The raw truth is that criticism, in all its forms, is an inevitable part of life.

If you've ever felt the cold dread of an impending critique or the hot flush of anger after an unfair assessment, you're not alone. Yet, learning to cope with criticism isn't just about survival; it's about thriving. Embracing criticism as a catalyst for growth is a cornerstone of maintaining confidence in challenging situations.

The Anatomy of Criticism

Before we can learn to cope with criticism, we must understand its various forms and motivations. Criticism isn't a monolithic entity; it comes in many flavours, each with its unique impact and purpose.

- **Constructive Criticism:** This is the gold standard of feedback. Offered with good intentions, it aims to help you improve. Constructive criticism is specific, actionable and focuses on your behaviour or output rather than your character.
- **Destructive Criticism:** This is the verbal equivalent of a sucker punch. It's personal, hurtful and often intended to demean or belittle. Destructive criticism can be a symptom of the critic's own insecurities or a deliberate attempt to undermine your confidence.
- **Misguided Criticism:** Sometimes, well-meaning people offer feedback based on inaccurate information or faulty assumptions. While their intentions may be good, the feedback itself can be off base and unhelpful.

- **Backhanded Criticism:** This is a passive-aggressive form of feedback, often disguised as a compliment. It leaves you feeling uneasy and unsure whether you've been praised or insulted.

The Emotional Toll of Criticism

Criticism, even when well-intentioned, can trigger a cascade of negative emotions. It's not uncommon to feel hurt, angry, defensive or ashamed after being criticized. These emotional responses are deeply rooted in our evolutionary past. In our ancestors' time, rejection from the group could mean isolation and death. Even today, our brains are wired to perceive social disapproval as a threat to our survival.

Research has shown that criticism activates the same areas of the brain as physical pain. This explains why a harsh word can feel like a punch to the gut. The emotional impact of criticism can linger long after the words have been spoken, affecting our self-esteem, motivation and overall well-being.

The Perils of Ignoring Criticism

It's tempting to dismiss criticism as irrelevant or unimportant, especially if it comes from a source we don't respect or if it's delivered in a hurtful way. However, ignoring criticism altogether can be detrimental to our growth and development. Even unfair or inaccurate criticism can contain a kernel of truth. By refusing to engage with feedback, we miss out on valuable opportunities to learn and improve.

Ignoring criticism can also lead to a spiral of negativity. If we allow hurtful words to fester in our minds, they can erode our confidence and create a self-fulfilling prophecy of failure. On the other hand, engaging with criticism, even when it's difficult, can help us gain a new perspective, challenge our assumptions and ultimately become more resilient and confident.

Strategies for Coping with Criticism

The key to maintaining confidence in challenging situations is not to avoid criticism altogether but to develop effective strategies for coping with it. Here are some practical tips:

- **Take a Deep Breath:** When faced with criticism, our immediate reaction is often to fight or flee. Before you respond, take a moment to collect your thoughts and calm your emotions. A few deep breaths can help you avoid saying or doing something you might regret later.
- **Listen Actively:** Pay attention to what the critic is saying, both verbally and non-verbally. Try to

understand their perspective, even if you disagree with their assessment. Ask clarifying questions if needed.

- **Assess the Validity:** Not all criticism is created equal. Consider the source, their intentions and the evidence they provide. Is the criticism specific, actionable and relevant to your goals?
- **Separate the Message from the Messenger:** Even if the criticism is delivered in a hurtful way, try to focus on the content of the message rather than the delivery. Remember, the critic's behaviour is a reflection of them, not you.
- **Seek Support:** If you're struggling to cope with criticism, don't hesitate to reach out to trusted friends, family members or a therapist. Talking about your feelings can help you gain perspective and develop coping mechanisms.
- **Choose Your Battles:** You don't have to respond to every criticism. If the feedback is clearly destructive or irrelevant, it's perfectly okay to let it go.
- **Learn from the Experience:** Even unfair criticism can be a learning opportunity. Reflect on what you can take away from the experience, even if it's just a lesson in how not to treat others.
- **Practise Self-Compassion:** Remember that you're human, and it's okay to make mistakes. Treat yourself with kindness and understanding, especially when you're feeling vulnerable.

By implementing these strategies, you can transform criticism from a source of anxiety into a tool for personal growth.

Stress Management Techniques

'The greatest weapon against stress is our ability to choose one thought over another.'

—William James

Stress, that familiar tightness in your chest, the racing thoughts, the knot in your stomach—it's an unwelcome companion on the journey of life. It's the body's natural response to demands, both real and perceived, and it can manifest in a multitude of ways, from physical ailments to emotional turmoil. While a certain level of stress can be motivating, chronic or overwhelming, it can undermine your confidence, erode your well-being and hinder your ability to navigate challenging situations.

The Toll of Unmanaged Stress

Stress isn't merely an emotional state; it has tangible consequences for your health and overall quality of life. Chronic stress has been linked to a range of physical ailments, including cardiovascular disease, high blood pressure, weakened immune function and even accelerated ageing. On the emotional front, stress can lead to anxiety, depression, irritability and difficulty concentrating. It can also disrupt your sleep patterns, appetite and relationships.

In the context of maintaining confidence in challenging situations, unmanaged stress can be particularly detrimental. It can cloud your judgement, amplify self-doubt and make it difficult to think clearly and make sound decisions. When stress takes the reins, your confidence can falter, leaving you feeling overwhelmed and ill-equipped to handle the challenges that come your way.

The Science of Stress

Understanding the science behind stress can empower you to manage it more effectively. When you encounter a stressor, your body initiates a cascade of physiological responses known as the 'fight-or-flight' response. This response is designed to prepare you to either confront the threat or flee from it.

During this response, your adrenal glands release stress hormones like cortisol and adrenaline, which increase your heart rate, blood pressure and breathing rate. Your muscles tense, senses sharpen and body prioritizes immediate survival over long-term health. While this response can be life-saving in acute situations, chronic activation of the stress response can have a detrimental impact on your well-being.

Your Stress Management Toolkit

Fortunately, you don't have to be a passive victim of stress. By developing a personalized stress management toolkit, you can regain control, build resilience and maintain your confidence even in the face of adversity. Here are some powerful techniques to incorporate into your toolkit:

- **Mindfulness and Meditation:** These practices involve paying non-judgemental attention to the present moment. Mindfulness can help you become more aware of your thoughts, emotions and bodily sensations, allowing you to respond to stressors with greater clarity and composure. Meditation, a form of mindfulness that involves focusing your attention on a single point, such as your breath, can help calm your mind and reduce anxiety.
- **Relaxation Techniques:** Deep breathing exercises, progressive muscle relaxation and visualization are all effective ways to counteract the physiological effects of stress. These techniques can help lower your heart rate, blood pressure and muscle tension, promoting a sense of calm and relaxation.
- **Physical Activity:** Regular exercise isn't just good for your physical health; it's also a potent stress reliever.

Exercise triggers the release of endorphins, natural mood boosters that can help alleviate stress and anxiety. Whether it's a brisk walk, a yoga class or a dance session, find an activity you enjoy and make it a part of your routine.

- **Social Support:** Connecting with loved ones and building strong social networks can provide a buffer against stress. Talking to a trusted friend, family member or therapist can help you process your emotions, gain perspective and receive valuable support.

- **Healthy Lifestyle Habits:** Adequate sleep, a balanced diet and moderation in alcohol and caffeine consumption are essential for stress management. These habits support your overall well-being and provide your body with the resources it needs to cope with stress effectively.

- **Time Management:** Feeling overwhelmed by a never-ending to-do list can be a major source of stress. Learning to prioritize tasks, set realistic goals and delegate when possible can help you regain control of your time and reduce stress levels.

- **Cognitive Restructuring:** Our thoughts have a powerful influence on our emotions. Cognitive restructuring involves identifying and challenging negative thought patterns that contribute to stress. By reframing these thoughts in a more positive and realistic light, you can change your emotional response to stressors.

- **Humour and Play:** Laughter is truly good medicine. Engaging in activities that bring you joy and laughter can help lighten your mood, reduce stress and boost your resilience.
- **Professional Help:** If you're struggling to manage stress on your own, don't hesitate to seek professional help. Therapists can teach you coping skills, help you identify the root causes of your stress and provide personalized guidance for managing it effectively.

Tailoring Your Toolkit

The key to successful stress management is finding the techniques that work best for you. Experiment with different approaches and create a personalized toolkit that you can rely on in challenging situations. Remember, stress management is an ongoing process. It's about building resilience, developing healthy habits and cultivating a positive mindset that can help you navigate life's inevitable ups and downs with confidence and grace.

Building Resilience

'The oak fought the wind and was broken, the willow bent when it must and survived.'
—Robert Jordan, *The Fires of Heaven*

Resilience isn't about being unbreakable. It's about bending without breaking, adapting to the relentless winds of change and challenge. In a world that throws curveballs at every turn, fostering resilience is not just beneficial—it's essential for maintaining confidence and thriving in the face of adversity.

The Anatomy of Resilience

Resilience is not a fixed trait but a dynamic process. It's a combination of:

- **Robustness:** The ability to withstand stress and pressure without succumbing to them.
- **Resourcefulness**: The capacity to find solutions and utilize available resources effectively.
- **Recovery:** The aptitude to bounce back from setbacks and regain momentum.
- **Adaptability:** The willingness to learn from experiences and adjust strategies accordingly.

These four pillars form the bedrock of resilience, allowing individuals to face challenges head-on, learn from their mistakes and emerge stronger than before.

The Science of Resilience

Resilience is not just a psychological concept; it's deeply rooted in our biology. When faced with stress, our bodies release cortisol, the 'stress hormone'. While some cortisol is necessary for survival, chronic stress can lead to elevated cortisol levels, which can have detrimental effects on our physical and mental health.

Resilient individuals, however, have developed mechanisms to regulate their stress responses. Their brains exhibit increased activity in the prefrontal cortex, the region responsible for decision-making, problem-solving and emotional regulation. This heightened activity allows them to assess situations objectively, manage their emotions and devise effective coping strategies.

Furthermore, studies have shown that resilient individuals possess greater neuroplasticity, the brain's ability to reorganize itself by forming new neural connections. This means they are better equipped to learn from their experiences, adapt to new situations and develop new skills.

Cultivating Resilience: Strategies for the Real World

Building resilience is not an overnight process. It requires consistent effort, self-reflection and a willingness to embrace discomfort. Here are some strategies to enhance your resilience:

- **Challenge Your Thoughts:** Negative thought patterns can exacerbate stress and hinder resilience. When faced with a challenge, ask yourself: 'Is this thought helpful? Is it accurate? Is there another way to look at this situation?' By challenging negative thoughts and reframing them in a more positive light, you can reduce stress and enhance your ability to cope.

- **Embrace Change:** Change is an inevitable part of life. Instead of resisting it, learn to embrace it as an opportunity for growth and development. By adapting to new situations and challenges, you can expand your skillset, broaden your perspectives and build resilience.

- **Practise Self-Care:** Taking care of your physical and mental health is crucial for resilience. Get enough sleep, eat a healthy diet, exercise regularly and engage in activities that bring you joy and relaxation. By prioritizing self-care, you can reduce stress, improve your mood and enhance your ability to cope with challenges.

- **Seek Support:** Building resilience does not mean going it alone. Reach out to friends, family, mentors or therapists for support and guidance. Talking about your struggles and seeking advice can provide valuable insights, reduce stress and enhance your resilience.

- **Celebrate Your Successes:** Acknowledge and celebrate your achievements, no matter how small. By recognizing your successes, you can boost your confidence, reinforce positive behaviours and build momentum for future challenges.

Resilience in Action: Real-World Examples

The world is replete with examples of individuals who have demonstrated remarkable resilience in the face of adversity. Malala Yousafzai, a Pakistani activist for female education, survived being shot in the head by the Taliban and went on to become the youngest Nobel Peace Prize laureate. J.K. Rowling, the author of the Harry Potter series, faced numerous rejections before finding a publisher and becoming a global phenomenon. Nelson Mandela, the South African anti-apartheid revolutionary and politician, endured twenty-seven years of imprisonment before becoming his country's first black president.

These individuals exemplify the power of resilience— the ability to overcome obstacles, persevere through adversity and emerge stronger than before. They inspire us to believe in our own potential, to face our challenges head-on and to never give up on our dreams.

Resilience is not a destination but a journey. It's about continuously learning, growing and adapting to the ever-changing landscape of life. By cultivating resilience, you can not only maintain confidence in challenging situations but also thrive and flourish in the face of adversity.

PART III

IMPACTFUL STORYTELLING

11

THE POWER OF STORYTELLING

Storytelling is a fundamental human activity that has been used for millennia to entertain, educate, preserve culture and connect with others. Stories have the power to transport us to different worlds, evoke emotions, challenge our perspectives and inspire action. They are a powerful tool for communication, persuasion and personal growth.

Why Stories Matter

'After nourishment, shelter, and companionship, stories are the thing we need most in the world.'

—Philip Pullman

This assertion may seem bold, perhaps even hyperbolic. But consider this: Stories have been the cornerstone of human connection since time immemorial. Cave paintings, oral traditions and written texts—all are manifestations of our innate need to narrate, share and understand through the lens of experience. We are, quite simply, hardwired for stories.

The Science Behind the Spell

Why do stories hold such sway over us? Neuroscience offers compelling insights. When we engage with a well-crafted narrative, our brains don't just passively receive information. They come alive, firing on multiple cylinders.

- **Dopamine:** The 'feel-good' neurotransmitter floods our system, creating a sense of pleasure and anticipation.
- **Oxytocin:** This 'bonding hormone' is released, fostering feelings of connection and empathy with characters and their experiences.
- **Mirror Neurons:** These specialized cells activate, allowing us to vicariously experience the emotions and sensations depicted in the story.

In essence, stories are not just entertainment. They are a potent cocktail of neurochemicals that can influence our thoughts, feelings and even actions.

The Evolutionary Advantage

Stories have served a vital function throughout human history. They have helped us make sense of the world, transmit knowledge, warn of dangers, reinforce social bonds and inspire action. In a sense, stories are the original virtual reality simulators, allowing us to explore possibilities and consequences without risking life and limb.

Stories as Social Glue

Consider the campfire tales of our ancestors. These stories were not just idle amusements. They were a way to share information about hunting strategies, warn of predators, celebrate heroes and pass down cultural values. Stories created a shared reality, a sense of belonging and a collective identity.

Even today, stories continue to bind us together. We gather around televisions, movie screens and computer monitors to share narratives that spark conversation, debate and emotional resonance. We discuss books, podcasts and news articles, weaving our own interpretations into the fabric of the story.

The Power of Persuasion

Stories are not just about connection. They are also a powerful tool of persuasion. A well-told story can change minds, influence behaviour and even inspire movements.

Think of Martin Luther King Jr's 'I Have a Dream' speech. It was not just a recitation of facts and figures. It was a story of hope, a vision of a better future, a call to action that galvanized a nation.

Stories work because they bypass our rational defences and speak directly to our emotions. They create empathy, build trust and make abstract concepts tangible and relatable.

The Story of Us

Perhaps the most profound reason why stories matter is that they help us understand ourselves. We are all, in a sense, the protagonists of our own stories. We make choices, face challenges, experience joys and sorrows and ultimately seek meaning in our lives.

Stories offer us a mirror to reflect on our own experiences, a compass to guide us through life's uncertainties and a source of inspiration to overcome obstacles. They remind us that we are not alone, that others have faced similar struggles and that hope is always possible.

Beyond Entertainment

While stories are often associated with entertainment, their impact extends far beyond mere amusement. They are a fundamental part of how we learn, communicate, connect and make sense of the world. They have the power to shape our beliefs, values and actions.

In the following chapters, we will explore the myriad ways in which stories influence our lives, from shaping our personal identities to driving social change. We will delve into the science of storytelling, the art of crafting compelling narratives and the ethical considerations of using stories responsibly.

A Call to Embrace the Power of Story

As we embark on this journey, I invite you to embrace the power of story. Whether you are a writer, a speaker, a leader or simply a curious human being, understanding the profound impact of stories can enrich your life and empower you to make a difference in the world.

The Neuroscience of Storytelling

> *'We are, as a species, addicted to story. Even when the body goes to sleep, the mind stays up all night, telling itself stories.'*
>
> —Jonathan Gottschall

There's an undeniable magic to storytelling that transcends cultures and generations. Why is it that a well-told tale can transport us to distant lands, evoke deep emotions and leave an enduring impact on our minds? The answer lies in the intricate dance between narratives and our brains, a phenomenon known as the neuroscience of storytelling.

Your Brain on Stories: A Symphony of Neural Activity

When you lose yourself in a story, your brain doesn't just passively absorb information. It becomes an active participant, firing neurons in harmony with the narrative's rhythm. This captivating process, often called neural coupling, is akin to your brain simulating the experiences described in the story. When a character walks through a forest, the regions of your brain associated with movement and sensory perception light up as if you were taking those steps yourself. This immersive experience is the bedrock of why stories feel so real and why their lessons linger long after the final page is turned.

The Chemistry of Connection: Hormones and Neurotransmitters

Storytelling doesn't just engage our brains; it triggers a cascade of biochemical reactions that influence our emotions and behaviours. When we encounter a compelling story, our brains release oxytocin, often dubbed the 'love hormone'. This neurochemical fosters feelings of trust, empathy and connection, strengthening our bonds with the characters and the narrative itself.

Cortisol, the stress hormone, also plays a role. A well-paced story with escalating tension and conflict can trigger cortisol release, heightening our focus and attention. This hormonal cocktail, along with dopamine's reward system, ensures that a good story is both captivating and memorable.

The Universal Language of Emotion

While the specifics of a story might vary, the emotions they evoke are remarkably universal. Whether it's the joy of victory, the sting of betrayal or the sorrow of loss, stories tap into a shared emotional landscape that transcends cultural boundaries. This universality is rooted in the brain's limbic system, a collection of structures responsible for processing emotions. When we encounter emotional moments in a story, the limbic system reacts as if we were experiencing those emotions first-hand, solidifying the story's impact.

Mirror Neurons: Empathy in Action

One of the most fascinating aspects of the neuroscience of storytelling is the role of mirror neurons. These specialized neurons fire both when we act and when we observe someone else doing the same action. In the context of stories, mirror neurons allow us to vicariously experience the emotions and actions of characters. When a protagonist faces a difficult challenge, our mirror neurons help us empathize with their struggle, as if we were facing it ourselves. This deep sense of connection fuels our investment in the story and its characters.

The Power of Transportation: Why We Lose Ourselves in Stories

Have you ever been so engrossed in a book or movie that you lost track of time? This phenomenon, known as transportation, is a testament to the power of storytelling to captivate our attention and transport us to another world. When we're transported into a story, our sense of self temporarily fades and we become fully immersed in the narrative's reality. This altered state of consciousness enhances our enjoyment of the story and deepens its impact on our thoughts and feelings.

Memory and Meaning-Making: Stories as Mental Schemas

Stories don't just entertain; they help us make sense of the world around us. Our brains are wired to organize information into mental frameworks called schemas. These schemas act as filters through which we interpret new experiences. Stories provide ready-made schemas, helping us categorize events, understand social dynamics and predict outcomes. By fitting new information into these pre-existing story structures, we can more easily comprehend and remember complex concepts.

The Evolution of Storytelling: From Campfires to Cinema Screens

Storytelling is not a modern invention; it's an ancient practice deeply ingrained in human nature. From prehistoric cave paintings to oral traditions passed down through generations, stories have always served as a means of communication, education and entertainment. The advent of written language, the printing press and eventually digital media have only expanded the reach and impact of storytelling.

The Future of Storytelling: Where Science and Art Converge

As our understanding of the brain deepens, so too does our appreciation for the power of storytelling. Today, researchers are exploring how stories can be leveraged to enhance learning, improve communication and even promote healing. Whether it's using narratives to explain complex scientific concepts or crafting compelling stories to raise awareness for social issues, the marriage of neuroscience and storytelling has the potential to transform how we connect with the world around us.

12

ELEMENTS OF A GREAT STORY

A great story is a captivating journey that transports readers to another world, evokes emotions, and leaves a lasting impact. It's a delicate balance of various elements that work together to create a memorable experience for the audience. In this section, we will discuss some key elements that make up a great story.

Structure: Beginning, Middle, End

'A story is a letter that the author writes to himself, to tell himself things he would be afraid to tell anyone else.'

—Carlos Ruiz Zafón

The Foundation: The Beginning

The beginning of a story is not merely an introduction; it's an invitation. It's the outstretched hand, beckoning the reader into a world yet unknown. It's the spark that ignites curiosity, the whisper that promises intrigue. In the literary realm, beginnings are as diverse as the stories they initiate.

- **The Hook:** Whether it's a startling revelation, a poignant question or a vivid description, the hook's sole purpose is to ensnare the reader's attention. It's the literary equivalent of a fishing line cast into the depths of the reader's mind, hoping to catch their interest. Consider the opening lines of George Orwell's *1984*: 'It was a bright cold day in April, and the clocks were striking thirteen.' This jarring detail instantly disrupts the reader's sense of normality, compelling them to delve deeper.

- **Introducing the Protagonist:** The protagonist is the heart of the story, the character through whose eyes we experience the unfolding events. A well-crafted introduction can establish their personality, motivations and the challenges they're likely to face. Think of Scout Finch in Harper Lee's *To Kill a Mockingbird*, whose childlike voice and inquisitive nature immediately endear her to the reader.

- **Setting the Scene:** The setting is more than just a backdrop; it's a character in its own right. Whether it's a bustling cityscape or a desolate wasteland, the setting can influence the mood, tone and even the plot of the story. J.R.R. Tolkien's meticulous descriptions of Middle-earth in *The Lord of the Rings* not only transport readers to another world but also provide crucial context for the epic struggle between good and evil.

- **Establishing the Conflict:** Conflict is the engine that drives the story forward. It can be internal (a character grappling with their own demons) or external (a battle against an adversary or a societal issue). Introducing the conflict early on creates a sense of anticipation and raises questions that the reader will eagerly seek answers to as the story progresses.

The Core: The Middle

If the beginning is the spark, the middle is the flame. It's where the story truly comes alive, where characters evolve, relationships deepen and the plot thickens. The middle is the longest and often the most complex part of a story, but it's also where the magic truly happens.

- **Rising Action:** As the story progresses, the stakes get higher, the challenges become more daunting and the tension escalates. This is the rising action, a series of events that build upon the conflict established in the beginning. Each event pushes the protagonist closer to their breaking point, testing their resolve and forcing them to make difficult choices.

- **Character Development:** In the crucible of conflict, characters are forged. Their flaws are exposed, strengths tested and motivations revealed. Through their actions, dialogue and interactions with other characters, we gain a deeper understanding of who they are and what they stand for. Katniss Everdeen's transformation from a protective sister to a symbol of rebellion in *The Hunger Games* is a prime example of how characters can evolve in response to adversity.

- **Subplots and Twists:** Subplots are secondary storylines that intertwine with the main plot, adding layers of complexity and intrigue to the narrative. They can explore different facets of the story's world, introduce new characters or provide unexpected twists and turns that keep the reader guessing. In *Game of Thrones*, the numerous subplots involving different families and factions contribute to the intricate tapestry of the story and create a sense of unpredictability.

- **Theme Exploration:** The middle is where the story's underlying themes begin to emerge. Themes are the universal ideas or messages that the author wants to convey through the narrative. They can be explored through the characters' experiences, the choices they make and the consequences they face. The theme of social injustice is woven throughout Harper Lee's *To Kill a Mockingbird*, as Scout witnesses the racism and prejudice that permeate her community.

The Culmination: The End

In the spirit of avoiding a traditional conclusion, let's reimagine the end not as a definitive finish line but as a transformative threshold. It's a point of no return, a moment of reckoning where the consequences of all that has transpired become clear. But instead of tying everything up neatly with a bow, let's leave the reader with lingering questions, unresolved emotions and a sense of anticipation for what might come next.

- **Climax:** The climax is the pinnacle of the story, the moment of greatest tension and conflict. It's where the protagonist faces their ultimate challenge, where the choices they've made and the actions they've taken culminate in a decisive confrontation. The climax can be a physical battle, an emotional showdown or a moral dilemma. In *Harry Potter and the Deathly Hallows*, the final duel between Harry and Voldemort is the culmination of years of conflict, a battle that will determine the fate of the wizarding world.

- **Resolution (Open-Ended):** Instead of a tidy resolution, consider leaving some threads dangling and some questions unanswered. This doesn't mean leaving the reader dissatisfied but rather inviting them to continue the story in their own minds.

- **Lingering Impact:** Even without a traditional conclusion, the end should leave a lasting impression on the reader. Think about the themes and messages you want to leave them with. In *To Kill a Mockingbird*, Scout's realization that 'people are people' and her newfound empathy towards Boo Radley linger long after the book is closed.

Remember that the end is not an end-point but a jumping-off point. It should inspire reflection, conversation and perhaps even action. As writers, we have the power to create transformative ends that resonate deeply with our readers. So don't be afraid to push boundaries, take risks and let your imagination run wild. The possibilities are endless, and the journey is just beginning.

Characters and Their Roles

'What is character but the determination of incident? What is incident but the illustration of character?'
—Henry James

In the grand symphony of storytelling, characters are not mere puppets on strings but the living, breathing heart that pumps life into the narrative. They are the vessels through which we explore the human condition, the mirrors reflecting our own triumphs and tribulations. In the intricate dance of plot, setting and theme, characters emerge as the driving force, the catalysts for conflict and the agents of change.

The Essence of Character

A well-crafted character is more than a name on a page; it is a multifaceted being with desires, fears, flaws and strengths. It is the embodiment of contradictions and complexities, a reflection of the human spirit in all its glorious messiness. To create compelling characters, we must delve deep into their psyche, understanding their motivations, their backstories and the forces that shape their choices.

The characters we create are not static entities; they are dynamic beings who evolve and transform as the story unfolds. Their journeys are marked by trials and tribulations, by moments of triumph and despair. It is through these experiences that they learn, grow and ultimately find their place in the world.

The Role of Characters in Storytelling

Characters play a pivotal role in the art of storytelling, serving as the vehicle through which we explore the themes and ideas that resonate with us. They are the conduits of emotion, the vessels through which we experience joy, sorrow, anger and fear. Through their actions and interactions, they reveal the underlying truths of the human experience, challenging us to question our own beliefs and values.

Characters are not isolated entities; they are part of a larger ensemble, each contributing to the overall narrative. Their relationships with one another are complex and multifaceted, filled with love, hate, loyalty and betrayal. It is through these relationships that we gain a deeper understanding of the characters themselves and the world in which they inhabit.

Types of Characters

The world of storytelling is populated by a diverse cast of characters, each with their own unique role to play.

- **The Protagonist:** The central figure of the story, the one whose journey we follow most closely. The protagonist is not necessarily a hero or a saint; they may be flawed, even morally ambiguous. But they are the characters with whom we identify most strongly, the ones whose fate we care about most deeply.

- **The Antagonist:** The force that opposes the protagonist, the obstacle standing in the way of their goals. The antagonist can take many forms: a villainous individual, a corrupt institution or even an internal struggle within the protagonists themselves.
- **Supporting Characters:** The individuals who surround the protagonist and antagonist, enriching the story with their own unique perspectives and experiences. Supporting characters can be allies, mentors, love interests, rivals or even enemies.

The Importance of Character Development

Character development is the process of creating believable and relatable characters, who evolve and change over the course of a story. It is a crucial element of storytelling, as it allows us to connect with the characters on a deeper level and invest in their journeys.

There are many ways to develop characters, including:

- **Backstory:** Exploring a character's past experiences and relationships can provide valuable insights into their motivations and behaviour.

- **Internal Conflict:** Characters who struggle with internal conflicts, such as moral dilemmas or personal demons, are often more compelling than those who are simply good or evil.
- **Relationships:** The way a character interacts with others can reveal much about their personality and values.
- **Growth and Change:** Characters who learn and grow over the course of a story are more satisfying than those who remain stagnant.

The Power of Character-Driven Stories

Character-driven stories are those in which the characters are the primary focus, rather than the plot or setting. These stories often explore complex themes and ideas through the lens of the characters' experiences. Some of the most beloved stories in literature and film are character-driven, including:

- *To Kill a Mockingbird*: This classic novel explores themes of racial injustice and moral courage through the eyes of Scout Finch, a young girl growing up in the American South.
- *The Godfather*: This epic film tells the story of the Corleone family, a powerful Mafia clan, and the complex relationships between its members.

- **The Lord of the Rings:** This fantasy trilogy follows the journey of Frodo Baggins, a hobbit who must destroy the One Ring, a powerful artefact that threatens to enslave all of Middle-earth.

These stories resonate with us because they offer a glimpse into the lives of characters who are both relatable and extraordinary. We see ourselves in their struggles and triumphs, and we are inspired by their courage and resilience.

Conflict and Resolution

'The test of a first-rate intelligence is the ability to hold two opposed ideas in mind at the same time and still retain the ability to function.' F. Scott Fitzgerald's words ring true not only in the realm of intellectual prowess but also in the heart of storytelling. It's in the clash of opposing forces—the conflict—that stories find their pulse, their tension and, ultimately, their resolution.

Consider this: a world without conflict is a world without stories. A story without conflict is a flatline on a heart monitor. It's the absence of life's vital signs, the denial of the human condition. We are creatures of contradictions, of desires and limitations, of aspirations and flaws. Our stories mirror these complexities, and conflict is the stage upon which these dramas unfold.

The Anatomy of Conflict

Conflict isn't merely a disagreement or a challenge; it's the engine that propels a story forward. It takes myriad forms, each leaving a distinct mark on the narrative landscape.

- **Internal Conflict:** This is the battle waged within a character's mind or heart. It's the struggle between competing desires, beliefs or values. A character may grapple with guilt, fear, ambition or the weight of a difficult decision. Internal conflict adds depth and complexity to characters, making them relatable and compelling.

- **External Conflict:** This is the clash between a character and an external force. It could be another character, a group of people, a natural disaster or even a societal norm. External conflict creates obstacles and raises the stakes, driving the plot forward.

- **Interpersonal Conflict:** This arises from the interactions between characters. It could be rivalry, a misunderstanding, a clash of personalities or a difference in goals. Interpersonal conflict fuels dramatic tension and reveals the characters' true nature.

- **Societal Conflict:** This stems from the tension between an individual and the broader society. It could be a fight for justice, a challenge to authority or a struggle against prejudice. Societal conflict often explores themes of power, inequality and social change.

The Art of Escalation

Conflict isn't static; it evolves and intensifies over the course of a story. The art of escalation lies in carefully raising the stakes, increasing the pressure on the characters and tightening the screws of tension. Each conflict should build upon the previous one, leading to a climactic confrontation.

Think of it as a symphony building to a crescendo. The initial notes introduce the melody, the subsequent movements develop it and the finale delivers a powerful resolution. Similarly, in a story, the conflicts start as subtle dissonances, gradually growing in intensity until they reach a point of no return.

The Crucible of Change

Conflict isn't merely a destructive force; it's a crucible of change. It tests the characters, pushing them to their limits, forcing them to make difficult choices and, ultimately, transforming them. It's through conflict that characters discover their strengths, confront their weaknesses and learn valuable lessons.

Think of the classic hero's journey. The hero sets out on a quest, encounters numerous obstacles and adversaries and, through these trials, grows in strength, wisdom and resilience. The conflict they face isn't merely a series of challenges; it's a transformative process.

The Dance of Resolution

Resolution isn't merely the end of a conflict; it's the culmination of a character's journey. It's the moment when they confront their fears, overcome their obstacles and emerge changed. Resolution can take many forms:

- **Victory:** The character achieves their goal, defeats their adversary or overcomes a personal challenge.
- **Compromise:** The character finds a middle ground, resolving the conflict through negotiation or sacrifice.
- **Acceptance:** The character comes to terms with a situation they cannot change, finding peace or understanding.
- **Loss:** The character experiences defeat or failure but learns a valuable lesson or gains a new perspective.

The key to a satisfying resolution is that it feels earned. It should be the natural outcome of the character's journey, the logical conclusion of their struggles. A contrived or deus ex machina resolution can leave the reader feeling cheated and unsatisfied.

Conflict and resolution are the yin and yang of storytelling. They are opposing forces that create dynamic tension, driving the narrative forward and transforming the characters. A well-crafted conflict is a crucible of change, a test of character and a catalyst for growth. A satisfying resolution is the culmination of a character's journey, the moment when they emerge from the fire, transformed and reborn.

Happy writing! So, keep exploring, keep writing and, most importantly, keep creating. Because in the end, it's not about how you finish your story but the impact it leaves on others that truly matters. Thank you for joining me on this journey through crafting a compelling ending. I hope these tips and insights have been helpful to you in your own writing process. Now, go forth and write an ending that will leave readers wanting more!

13

CRAFTING YOUR STORY

Crafting your story involves shaping your personal or professional experiences into a narrative that resonates with others. Whether you're aiming to write a memoir, deliver a captivating presentation or create an impactful personal brand, storytelling is an essential skill to master. In this section, we'll explore tips and techniques for crafting your story compellingly and authentically.

Finding Your Voice

> 'The difference between the right word and the almost right word is the difference between lightning and a lightning bug.'
>
> —Mark Twain

The words of Mark Twain, a master storyteller, ring especially true when we consider the concept of 'voice' in writing. It's that elusive quality that makes a story uniquely yours, the lightning that illuminates your narrative and sets it apart from the rest.

The Essence of Voice

Voice is not merely the words you choose, but the soul behind those words. It's the melody that resonates throughout your writing, the rhythm that sets the pace of your story. It's the emotional resonance, the underlying message and the unique perspective you bring to the table.

Your voice is an amalgamation of your personality, experiences, beliefs and values. It's the fingerprint you leave on every sentence, the distinct flavour that lingers in the reader's mind long after they've finished your story.

The Importance of Voice in Crafting Your Story

Why is a voice so important in crafting your story? Because it's the bridge that connects you to your reader. It's the invisible thread that weaves through your narrative, pulling the reader in and keeping them engaged.

A strong voice creates an emotional connection with the reader. It makes them feel like they're not just reading a story but experiencing it alongside the characters. It draws them into the world you've created and makes them invested in the outcome.

Moreover, a distinctive voice sets your story apart from the countless others vying for the reader's attention. It's your unique selling point, the reason why a reader would choose your story over another.

The Journey of Finding Your Voice

Finding your voice is not a destination, but a journey. It's an ongoing process of self-discovery, experimentation and refinement. There's no magic formula, no one-size-fits-all approach. It's a personal quest, as unique as you are.

The first step in this journey is self-awareness. To find your voice, you need to understand who you are as a writer. What are your strengths and weaknesses? What are your passions and interests? What are your values and beliefs?

The next step is experimentation. Don't be afraid to try different styles, genres and formats. Play with language, experiment with different voices and see what resonates with you.

Feedback is crucial in this process. Share your work with others and get their honest opinions. Listen to their critiques, but don't let them stifle your creativity. Use their feedback as a tool to hone your craft and develop your voice.

The Challenges of Finding Your Voice

Finding your voice is not always easy. It can be a frustrating and discouraging process. You may face self-doubt, writer's block and the pressure to conform to societal expectations.

One of the biggest challenges is the fear of being judged. It's easy to get caught up in what others think, to try to please everyone and end up pleasing no one. Remember, your voice is yours and yours alone. Don't let anyone else tell you how to sound.

Another challenge is the tendency to imitate others. It's natural to be inspired by other writers, but don't let their voices overshadow yours. Use their work as a springboard, not a blueprint.

The Rewards of Finding Your Voice

The journey of finding your voice may be challenging, but the rewards are immeasurable. When you find your voice, you unlock your full potential as a writer. You become more confident, more authentic and more expressive.

Your writing becomes more engaging, more impactful and more memorable. You connect with your readers on a deeper level, and your stories resonate with them long after they've finished reading.

Finding your voice is not just about improving your writing, it's about personal growth. It's about discovering who you are, what you stand for and what you have to offer the world. It's about finding your place in the literary landscape and making your mark.

Tailoring Stories to Your Audience

> 'The storyteller is an alchemist, transforming the raw materials of life into golden narratives that illuminate the human experience.'
>
> —Unknown

Every story has the potential to be a masterpiece, but like a sculptor carefully selecting the right tools for their medium, the storyteller must carefully consider their audience to truly bring their vision to life. In this chapter, we embark on an exploration of audience alchemy, the process of understanding, engaging and, ultimately, captivating readers by tailoring stories to their unique tastes and desires.

Deciphering the Audience Code

Imagine stepping into a grand library, each shelf brimming with stories from every genre imaginable. Just as you would instinctively gravitate towards sections that align with your personal interests, your audience is drawn to stories that resonate with their experiences, beliefs and aspirations. By understanding your readers on a deeper level, you unlock the power to craft stories that not only entertain but also forge lasting connections.

1. The Demographics Dance

The most fundamental step in audience alchemy is understanding the demographic make-up of your readership. Age, gender, cultural background, education level and socio-economic status are all threads in the intricate tapestry of audience identity. Consider how a story about teenage love might resonate differently with a group of middle-aged readers versus a younger audience. By tailoring your language, themes and even character development to align with demographic nuances, you ensure that your story speaks directly to the hearts and minds of your intended readers.

2. Psychographics: Peering into the Soul of Your Audience

While demographics provide a snapshot of your audience, psychographics delve deeper into their attitudes, values, interests and lifestyles. What are their hopes, fears and dreams? What causes do they support? What kind of humour do they enjoy? By crafting stories that reflect their inner worlds, you create an instant sense of kinship and understanding. Imagine a story about environmental activism resonating more deeply with readers who prioritize sustainability and ecological responsibility. By aligning your narrative with their core beliefs, you not only entertain but also inspire and empower.

3. The Genre Gauntlet

Genre is another key ingredient in the audience's alchemy formula. Each genre comes with its own set of expectations, tropes and conventions. Readers of fantasy expect dragons and magic, while those drawn to thrillers crave suspense and unexpected twists. By adhering to genre conventions while infusing your unique voice and perspective, you create a reading experience that is both familiar and refreshing.

4. The Platform Puzzle

In today's digital age, the platform on which your story is shared plays a pivotal role in shaping audience engagement. A short story published on a social media platform might require a snappier pace and a more concise narrative structure than a novel serialized on a dedicated reading app. By tailoring your writing style and formatting to suit the platform, you optimize the reader experience and maximize engagement.

The Art of Adaptation

Once you have a firm grasp of your audience, the next step is to adapt your story to their specific tastes and expectations. This involves not only adjusting language and themes but also making subtle shifts in character development, plot structure and even the overall tone of your narrative.

1. Language as a Bridge

Language is the primary tool through which you communicate with your readers. By using vocabulary, idioms and references that resonate with your audience, you create a sense of familiarity and connection. A story intended for a younger audience might use more colloquial language and pop culture references, while a story for an older demographic might employ a more formal or sophisticated tone. By tailoring your language to suit your readers, you ensure that your message is not only understood but also embraced.

2. Themes That Touch the Heart

Themes are the beating heart of your story, the underlying messages that resonate with readers long after they've turned the final page. By selecting themes that align with your audience's values and interests, you forge a deeper connection that transcends mere entertainment. A story about overcoming adversity might resonate more deeply with readers who have faced challenges in their own lives, while a story about finding love might strike a chord with those seeking romance and connection.

3. Characters as Mirrors

Characters are the vessels through which readers experience your story. By crafting characters that your audience can relate to, you create a sense of empathy and investment. Consider the demographics and psychographics of your readers when developing your characters' personalities, backgrounds and motivations. By creating characters who mirror their readers' experiences and aspirations, you invite them to become active participants in your narrative.

Incorporating Personal Experiences

'The universe is made of stories, not atoms.'

—Muriel Rukeyser

Ever listened to a captivating speaker and wondered, 'How do they do it?' Their words flow effortlessly, their stories resonate deeply and their presence commands attention. More often than not, the secret ingredient is their willingness to share authentic personal experiences. In this chapter of 'Crafting Your Story', we delve into the transformative power of incorporating lived experiences into your narrative. We'll explore how personal anecdotes can breathe life into your message, forge stronger connections with your audience and, ultimately, elevate your story to new heights.

Why Personal Experiences Matter

Storytelling is an ancient art form, a fundamental way humans connect and communicate. We're hardwired to respond to narratives that evoke emotions, challenge our perspectives and offer a glimpse into the lives of others. When you infuse your story with personal experiences, you tap into this innate human desire for connection.

- **Authenticity:** In a world saturated with information and opinions, authenticity is a rare and valuable commodity. Sharing your personal journey, complete with its triumphs and tribulations, is a powerful way to establish trust and credibility with your audience. It shows that you're not just another talking head but a real person with real experiences.

- **Relatability:** Everyone loves a good story, and personal anecdotes are often the most relatable kind. When you share your struggles, your victories or even your embarrassing moments, you create a sense of common ground with your audience. They see themselves in your story, and that connection fosters a deeper engagement with your message.

- **Emotional Impact:** Facts and figures can inform, but stories have the power to move people. Personal experiences are rich in emotions, from joy and excitement to sadness and fear. By tapping into these emotions, you create a visceral experience for your audience, making your story more memorable and impactful.

- **Persuasion:** When you want to persuade someone, logic alone isn't always enough. Stories, especially those rooted in personal experience, can be incredibly persuasive. They appeal to our emotions and values, making your message more compelling and convincing.

Weaving Personal Experiences Into Your Narrative

Now that we understand the significance of personal experiences, let's explore how to seamlessly integrate them into your story.

- **Choose Relevant Experiences:** Not every personal anecdote is suitable for every story. Carefully select experiences that align with your overall message and resonate with your target audience. Consider the emotions you want to evoke and the points you want to emphasize.

- **Show, Don't Tell:** Don't just summarize your experiences; bring them to life with vivid details and sensory language. Describe the sights, sounds, smells, tastes and textures that made the experience memorable. Paint a picture in the minds of your audience.

- **Embrace Vulnerability:** Don't shy away from sharing your vulnerabilities and imperfections. These are the elements that make your story authentic and relatable. Talk about your fears, your failures and the lessons you learnt along the way.

- **Connect the Dots:** Explain how your personal experiences shaped your beliefs, values or actions. Draw a clear line between your past and your present, showing how your journey has led you to where you are today.

- **Use Storytelling Techniques:** Employ classic storytelling techniques like conflict, resolution and character development. Structure your anecdotes with a clear beginning, middle and end. Build suspense and keep your audience engaged.

Examples of Personal Experiences in Storytelling

Let's look at a few examples of how personal experiences can be incorporated into different types of stories:

- **Memoir:** Memoirs are inherently personal, drawing heavily on the author's life experiences. A well-crafted memoir can transport readers to another time and place, allowing them to vicariously experience the author's journey.
- **Business Presentations:** A dry business presentation can be transformed into a captivating story by incorporating personal anecdotes. Sharing stories about customer interactions, product development challenges or personal career milestones can make your message more engaging and memorable.
- **Public Speaking:** Whether you're giving a TED Talk or a keynote address, personal stories can add depth and authenticity to your presentation. They can illustrate complex concepts, inspire action and create a lasting connection with your audience.
- **Social Media:** Even in the fast-paced world of social media, personal experiences can shine. Sharing snippets of your life, thoughts and experiences can help you build a loyal following and establish yourself as a relatable and trustworthy voice.

The Art of Authenticity

Incorporating personal experiences into your story is an art, not a science. There are no hard and fast rules, but there is one cardinal rule: be authentic. Don't embellish or exaggerate your experiences for the sake of a good story. Your audience will appreciate your honesty and vulnerability.

Remember, your story is unique. Your experiences, your perspectives and your voice are what make your narrative compelling. By embracing your personal journey and sharing it with the world, you have the power to inspire, educate and entertain. So, go forth and craft your story with authenticity, passion and the rich tapestry of your lived experience.

14

TECHNIQUES FOR IMPACTFUL STORYTELLING

Impactful storytelling hinges on several key techniques that can captivate and resonate with an audience. Firstly, understanding your audience is crucial; knowing their interests, values and pain points allows you to tailor the story in a way that is relevant and engaging for them. Secondly, starting with a strong hook can grab the audience's attention right from the beginning. This could be a provocative question, a striking fact or an emotional anecdote. Additionally, creating vivid and relatable characters helps to humanize your story and connect with the audience on a personal level. Using sensory details and descriptive language can also make the narrative more immersive and memorable.

In this section, we will delve deeper into these techniques and explore how you can use them to craft a compelling and impactful story.

Using Descriptive Language

> *'The difference between the almost right word and the right word is really a large matter—it's the difference between the lightning bug and the lightning.'*
>
> —Mark Twain

Twain's quote serves as an electrifying reminder of the potency contained within language. In the realm of storytelling, words aren't merely vehicles for information; they are pigments, sounds, textures and tastes. They are the tools with which we sculpt vivid worlds and breathe life into characters. In this chapter, we'll delve into the artistry of descriptive language—unravelling its power to elevate your narratives from the mundane to the extraordinary.

Evoking Sensory Experiences: A Symphony for the Senses

Imagine a scene: a bustling marketplace in a faraway land. The air is thick with the aroma of exotic spices, the vibrant hues of silk fabrics shimmer in the sunlight and the cacophony of voices bargaining in a foreign tongue fills your ears. Now, strip away the sensory details—the smells, sights and sounds. What remains is a skeletal outline, devoid of the rich tapestry that makes the scene come alive.

Descriptive language operates on the principle of immersion. It invites your readers to step into the world you've created, not as passive observers but as active participants. By engaging their senses, you forge a visceral connection that transcends the limitations of the written word.

- **Sight:** Describe the play of light on a character's face, the intricate patterns of a mosaic floor or the majestic sweep of a mountain range.
- **Sound:** Capture the rustle of leaves in the wind, the creak of an old wooden door or the roar of a crowd at a sporting event.
- **Touch:** Convey the softness of a feather, the roughness of tree bark or the chill of a winter's night.
- **Taste:** Describe the tang of a lemon, the sweetness of honey or the bitterness of coffee.
- **Smell:** Evoke the fragrance of blooming flowers, the aroma of freshly baked bread or the stench of a swamp.

By weaving these sensory details into your prose, you create a multilayered experience that resonates with your readers on a deeper level.

Show, Don't Tell: Unleashing the Power of Imagination

'The difference between the right word and the almost right word is the difference between lightning and a lightning bug.'

—Mark Twain

The adage 'show, don't tell' reigns supreme. It's the guiding principle that separates the amateur from the virtuoso. Instead of simply stating that a character is angry, describe their clenched fists, flushed face and the venomous words that spew forth from their lips.

Instead of merely informing your readers that a place is beautiful, paint a picture of sun-dappled meadows, crystal-clear streams and majestic peaks piercing the sky.

Showing, rather than telling, empowers your readers to become co-creators of your narrative. By providing them with the raw materials of sensory details, you allow their imaginations to fill in the gaps, resulting in a more immersive and personalized experience.

The Magic of Metaphor and Simile: Painting with Words

Metaphors and similes are the painter's brushstrokes, adding depth, texture and vibrancy to your writing. They allow you to transcend the literal and venture into the realm of the figurative, creating connections between disparate ideas and objects.

A well-crafted metaphor can illuminate a character's inner turmoil like a dark cloud obscuring the sun. A clever simile can capture the essence of a setting, comparing a bustling city to a beehive. These linguistic devices inject your writing with a sense of wonder and surprise, leaving your readers pondering the nuances of your words long after they've finished reading.

Beyond the Basics: Advanced Techniques for Wordsmiths

While sensory details, showing vs telling and metaphors are essential tools in the descriptive writer's arsenal, there are more advanced techniques that can elevate your prose to new heights:

- **Personification:** Breathe life into inanimate objects by imbuing them with human characteristics. Imagine a house that sighs with relief as the last guest departs, or a river that whispers secrets to the trees along its banks.
- **Symbolism:** Use objects, characters or events to represent abstract ideas or concepts. A wilting flower might symbolize the fragility of life, while a raven could signify impending doom.

- **Allusion:** Reference well-known works of literature, art, or music to enrich your writing and create a sense of shared cultural understanding. A character's tragic downfall might evoke Shakespeare's *Macbeth*, while a breathtaking landscape might conjure up images of Monet's water lilies.

By experimenting with these advanced techniques, you can add layers of complexity and intrigue to your narratives, captivating your readers and leaving a lasting impression.

The Power of Precision: Choosing the Right Words

Every word in your story should serve a purpose. Avoid generic adjectives like 'nice', 'good' or 'bad'. Instead, opt for specific, evocative words that paint a vivid picture in your reader's mind. A character isn't simply 'sad'; they are 'melancholy', 'despondent' or 'grief-stricken'. A house isn't merely 'old'; it is 'dilapidated', 'crumbling' or 'haunted by the ghosts of its past'.

By choosing your words with care, you imbue your writing with a sense of precision and artistry. Your readers will feel the weight of each syllable, the nuance of each phrase and the power of each sentence.

Descriptive language is not merely about adornment; it is the lifeblood of your story. It is the tool with which you transport your readers to new worlds, introduce them to unforgettable characters and leave them breathless with anticipation. By mastering the art of description, you unlock the full potential of your storytelling prowess.

Incorporating Emotion

'The most powerful person in the world is the storyteller.'
—Steve Jobs

Stories are the lifeblood of human connection. They transcend time, culture and language, weaving a tapestry of shared experience that binds us together. But what makes a story truly unforgettable? What separates a good story from a great one? The answer lies in the heart of every narrative: emotion.

Emotional connection is the holy grail of storytelling. It's what transforms a collection of words into a living, breathing entity that resonates with readers on a deep, visceral level. It's what makes us laugh, cry, fear and hope alongside the characters we encounter. And it's what keeps us turning pages long after the lights should have been turned out.

The Science Behind Emotional Storytelling

Our brains are wired for stories. We're neurologically programmed to respond to narrative, to seek out patterns and meaning in the chaos of our lives. When we encounter a story, our brains release a cocktail of chemicals that heighten our engagement and immersion. Dopamine, the 'feel-good' neurotransmitter, floods our system, rewarding us for paying attention. Oxytocin, the 'love hormone', strengthens our empathy and connection to the characters. Cortisol, the stress hormone, keeps us on the edge of our seats.

But the most powerful chemical of all is perhaps the most unexpected: tears. When we cry, our bodies release endorphins, natural painkillers that induce a sense of calm and well-being. This is why we often feel better after a good cry, and why emotionally charged stories can have such a profound impact on us.

The Art of Emotional Alchemy

Incorporating emotion into your storytelling is a delicate art. It requires a deep understanding of human psychology, a keen eye for detail and a willingness to experiment and take risks. Here are a few techniques you can use to infuse your stories with emotional power:

- **Show, Don't Tell:** One of the cardinal rules of storytelling is to show, not tell. This means using vivid language, sensory details and concrete actions to bring your characters' emotions to life. Don't just tell us your character is sad; show us their slumped shoulders, their tear-stained cheeks, their trembling hands.

- **Tap into Universal Themes:** The most powerful emotions are those that resonate with everyone, regardless of background or experience. Love, loss, fear, hope, joy, anger—these are the raw materials of human existence. By tapping into these universal themes, you can create stories that touch the hearts of readers from all walks of life.

- **Create Conflict and Tension:** Conflict is the engine that drives every story. It creates tension, raises stakes and forces characters to make difficult choices. By weaving conflict into your narrative, you can heighten emotional intensity and keep readers on the edge of their seats.

- **Use Sensory Details:** Our senses are our gateway to the world. By using sensory details to describe sights, sounds, smells, tastes and textures, you can immerse readers in your story and make them feel like they're right there alongside your characters.

- **Master the Art of Pacing:** Pacing is the rhythm of your story. It's the ebb and flow of tension and release, the balance of action and introspection. By mastering the art of pacing, you can control the emotional roller coaster of your narrative and keep readers engaged from beginning to end.

The Power of Emotional Resonance

Emotional resonance is the ultimate goal of storytelling. It's the feeling that a story has touched us on a deep, personal level, that it has changed us in some small but meaningful way. When a story resonates with us, we carry it with us long after we've finished reading it. We think about it, we talk about it and we recommend it to our friends.

Emotional resonance is what makes a story truly unforgettable. It's what transforms a good story into a great one. And it's what keeps us coming back to stories again and again, seeking out that spark of connection, that glimmer of hope, that reminder that we are not alone.

The Role of Timing and Pacing

'Great storytelling is not about the length of the road, but the scenery along the way.'

—Unknown

Imagine a world where music lacked rhythm, where paintings lacked contrast, where dance lacked movement. It would be a lifeless, monotonous existence. Storytelling, too, requires a dynamic interplay of elements to captivate an audience. In the realm of impactful narratives, timing and pacing are the unsung heroes, the heartbeat that infuses life and energy into your words.

The Symphony of Time

Timing, in essence, is the art of choosing the right moment to reveal information, introduce characters or escalate conflict. It's about understanding the emotional impact of events and orchestrating them to create a symphony of suspense, surprise and satisfaction.

Consider the classic thriller. The author doesn't reveal the killer in the first chapter; that would be a premature climax. Instead, they sprinkle clues, build tension and allow the reader's anticipation to simmer until the perfect moment for the big reveal arrives. This strategic timing transforms a mere plot point into a heart-pounding climax.

Pacing, on the other hand, is the rhythm of your narrative, the ebb and flow of action and reflection. It's the difference between a leisurely stroll through a scenic landscape and a breathless sprint to the finish line. Pacing controls the speed at which your story unfolds, ensuring that readers are neither bored by sluggishness nor overwhelmed by a relentless onslaught of events.

The Dance of Tension and Release

Effective storytelling is a dance between tension and release. Tension is the anticipation, the curiosity, the unease that keeps readers glued to the page. The release is the satisfaction of resolution, the answer to a burning question, the calming of troubled waters.

Masterful storytellers understand how to build tension through foreshadowing, cliffhangers and escalating stakes. They know when to tighten the screws and when to offer a moment of respite. This dynamic interplay of tension and release creates an emotional roller coaster that keeps readers engaged and invested in the outcome.

Think of a suspenseful scene in a movie. The music swells, the camera zooms in on a menacing figure lurking in the shadows and the protagonist's heart pounds in their chest. This is tension at its peak. Then, the figure steps into the light, revealing themselves to be a harmless passer-by. The music softens, the protagonist breathes a sigh of relief and the audience relaxes. This is release, and it's just as crucial to the storytelling experience as the tension that preceded it.

The Toolbox of Timing and Pacing

Storytellers have a wide array of tools at their disposal to manipulate timing and pacing:

- **Sentence Structure:** Short, staccato sentences can convey urgency, while long, flowing sentences can create a sense of reflection or introspection.

- **Word Choice:** Vivid verbs and evocative adjectives can quicken the pace, while descriptive passages can slow it down.
- **Scene Length:** A rapid succession of short scenes can accelerate the action, while a single, extended scene can delve deeper into character development or emotional nuance.
- **Dialogue:** Snappy back-and-forth dialogue can create a sense of immediacy, while monologues can offer insights into a character's thoughts and feelings.
- **White Space:** Strategic use of white space can signal a change in pace or a shift in focus.
- **Chapter Breaks:** Chapter breaks can be used to create cliffhangers, change perspectives or jump forward in time.

The key is to experiment with these tools and discover what works best for your particular story and your unique voice.

The Art of Adaptation

Timing and pacing are not one-size-fits-all. What works for one genre or audience may not work for another. For example, a fast-paced thriller might demand a breakneck pace with frequent cliffhangers, while a literary novel might benefit from a more leisurely pace that allows for deeper character exploration.

It's also important to adapt your timing and pacing to the specific scene or moment within your story. A pivotal revelation might warrant a slower pace to allow its impact to sink in, while a climactic battle might call for a rapid-fire succession of events to heighten the tension.

The Ultimate Goal: Emotional Resonance

The ultimate goal of mastering timing and pacing is to create emotional resonance with your readers. You want them to feel the excitement, the fear, the joy, the sorrow that your characters experience. You want them to be so invested in the story that they can't put the book down.

15

STORYTELLING IN DIFFERENT CONTEXTS

Storytelling is a fundamental human activity that transcends cultures and time periods. It is the art of conveying events, experiences or ideas through narratives.

Whether it's a simple anecdote shared among friends or an epic saga passed down through generations, storytelling serves to entertain, educate, preserve cultural heritage and connect people on a deeper level.

Personal Life: Connecting with Friends and Family

'Call it a clan, call it a network, call it a tribe, call it a family. Whatever you call it, whoever you are, you need one.'

—Jane Howard

The bonds of family and friendship aren't merely threads in the fabric of our lives; they are the very loom upon which the tapestry of our existence is woven.

They provide the warmth of belonging, the joy of shared experiences and the sturdy foundation upon which we build our lives. In an era where digital connections often overshadow face-to-face interactions, the importance of nurturing these real-world relationships cannot be overstated.

Family: The Cradle of Connection

Family is the first and most fundamental social unit in human society. It's where we first learn about love, trust, communication and conflict resolution. The stories we hear, the traditions we observe and the values we inherit from our families shape our identities and influence the choices we make throughout our lives.

Beyond the Bloodline: The Power of Chosen Family

For many, the concept of family extends beyond blood ties. Friends who become like siblings, mentors who become like parents and communities that offer a sense of belonging can all be considered part of our chosen family.

These relationships are forged through shared experiences, mutual respect and unwavering support.

The Art of Maintaining Family Connections

Nurturing family relationships requires effort and intentionality. Here are a few strategies for strengthening the bonds that tie you to your loved ones:

- **Prioritize Quality Time:** Schedule regular family gatherings, game nights or movie marathons. These shared experiences create lasting memories and foster a sense of togetherness.
- **Open Communication:** Encourage open and honest communication within your family. Create a safe space where everyone feels comfortable expressing their thoughts, feelings and concerns.
- **Show Appreciation:** Express your love and appreciation for your family members regularly. A simple 'thank you' or 'I love you' can go a long way in strengthening emotional connections.

Friendship: The Glue of Life

Friends are the family we choose. They are the people who know us best, who celebrate our victories and who offer a shoulder to lean on during challenging times. True friendships are built on trust, loyalty and shared values.

Cultivating Meaningful Friendships

Building and maintaining strong friendships requires effort and dedication. Here are some tips for cultivating meaningful connections with your friends:

- **Be Present:** Put away your phone and be fully present when spending time with your friends. Listen actively, show empathy and engage in meaningful conversations.
- **Offer Support:** Be there for your friends during both good times and bad. Celebrate their achievements, offer a listening ear when they're struggling and provide practical assistance when needed.
- **Forgive and Forget:** No friendship is perfect. Misunderstandings and disagreements are inevitable. Learn to forgive and forget and focus on the positive aspects of your relationships.

The Importance of Balancing Family and Friendship

Both family and friendship play vital roles in our lives, and it's essential to strike a healthy balance between the two. While family provides a sense of belonging and unconditional love, friendships offer companionship, support and diverse perspectives.

Professional Life: Presentations and Pitches

'Call it a clan, call it a network, call it a tribe, call it a family. Whatever you call it, whoever you are, you need one.'

—Jane Howard

In a world that often pulls us in a thousand directions, the bonds we share with friends and family remain a constant source of strength, joy and belonging. These relationships form the bedrock of our personal lives, shaping who we are and how we experience the world. Storytelling plays a pivotal role in nurturing and strengthening these connections, allowing us to share experiences, create shared memories and forge deeper understanding.

The Power of Shared Narratives

Imagine a family gathered around a crackling fireplace, each member taking turns to recount tales of their day, their dreams or their childhood escapades. Or picture a group of friends reminiscing about a shared adventure, their laughter echoing through the room as they embellish details and relive cherished moments. These are the scenes where stories weave their magic, binding individuals together in a tapestry of shared experiences.

Storytelling within the context of family and friendships serves several vital functions:

- **Strengthening Bonds:** When we share stories with loved ones, we invite them into our inner world, revealing our thoughts, feelings and experiences. This act of vulnerability fosters trust and intimacy, strengthening the emotional connection between individuals.

- **Creating Shared Memories:** Stories have the power to transport us back in time, allowing us to relive moments of joy, laughter and even sadness. When we share these memories with others, we create a collective narrative that strengthens the bond between us.

- **Passing on Traditions and Values:** Family stories often carry with them a rich history of traditions, values and cultural heritage. By sharing these stories, we ensure that these important aspects of our identity are passed down through generations.

- **Providing Support and Comfort:** In times of difficulty, stories can offer solace and support. Sharing our struggles with friends and family can help us feel less alone and more understood.

The Art of Storytelling in Personal Relationships

While storytelling comes naturally to most of us, there are ways to enhance the impact of our narratives and make them more engaging for our loved ones:

- **Be Authentic:** The most powerful stories are those that come from the heart. Share your experiences honestly and openly, without fear of judgement.
- **Use Vivid Details:** Bring your stories to life by using descriptive language that appeals to the senses. Describe the sights, sounds, smells and tastes that make your experiences unique.
- **Embrace Humour:** Laughter is a universal language that can bridge gaps and create connections. Don't be afraid to inject humour into your stories, even when recounting difficult experiences.
- **Be a Good Listener:** Storytelling is a two-way street. Show genuine interest in the stories of your friends and family members. Ask questions, offer encouragement and validate their experiences.

Storytelling Across Generations

One of the most beautiful aspects of storytelling within families is its ability to bridge generational gaps. Grandparents sharing tales of their youth with their grandchildren can create a sense of continuity and connection that transcends time. These stories can offer valuable insights into the past, guide the future and strengthen the bond between generations.

In an age where technology often dominates our communication, making time for face-to-face storytelling with loved ones is more important than ever. Put away the distractions, gather around a table and let the stories flow. The memories you create will be cherished for years to come.

Family Storytelling Traditions

Many families have unique storytelling traditions that have been passed down through generations. These traditions can take many forms, such as:

- **Family Dinner Stories:** Sharing stories around the dinner table is a classic way to connect with loved ones and learn about each other's lives.
- **Bedtime Stories:** Reading or telling stories to children at bedtime is a cherished ritual that fosters imagination, creativity and emotional bonding.
- **Family Reunions:** These gatherings often provide an opportunity to share stories and reconnect with relatives who may live far away.
- **Family Photo Albums**: Looking through old photos and sharing the stories behind them can be a nostalgic and meaningful way to connect with family history.

By embracing these traditions and creating new ones, we can ensure that the art of storytelling continues to thrive within our families.

Social Media and Digital Storytelling

'The universe is made of stories, not of atoms.'

—Muriel Rukeyser

In our increasingly interconnected world, social media platforms have emerged as the modern-day equivalent of the campfire, a virtual gathering space where stories are shared, connections are forged and communities are built. The rise of social media has revolutionized the way we tell stories, offering unprecedented opportunities for individuals and brands to connect with audiences on a global scale.

The Evolution of Storytelling in the Digital Age

Storytelling is an ancient human tradition, dating back to the earliest cave paintings and oral narratives. It is through stories that we make sense of the world, connect with others and transmit cultural values. The advent of digital technologies, particularly social media, has fundamentally transformed the landscape of storytelling, ushering in a new era of possibilities.

Social media platforms like Facebook, Instagram, X (formerly Twitter) and TikTok have democratized storytelling, empowering anyone with a smartphone and an Internet connection to become a content creator.

This has led to an explosion of user-generated content, ranging from personal anecdotes and travelogues to social commentary and political activism.

The Power of Visual Storytelling

One of the most significant ways social media has influenced storytelling is through the emphasis on visual content. Platforms like Instagram and Pinterest are built around images and videos, encouraging users to tell stories through compelling visuals. This has led to the rise of 'micro-stories', short-form narratives that capture attention in a matter of seconds.

The popularity of visual storytelling can be attributed to several factors. First, visuals are inherently more engaging than text, as they appeal to our emotions and imagination. Second, visuals are more easily shareable and consumable, making them ideal for the fast-paced nature of social media. Finally, visuals can transcend language barriers, allowing stories to be shared and understood by people from diverse cultural backgrounds.

Social Media as a Catalyst for Social Change

Social media has also proven to be a powerful tool for social change. The #MeToo movement, for example, gained momentum through the sharing of personal stories on social media, leading to widespread awareness and accountability for sexual harassment and assault. Similarly, the Black Lives Matter movement has utilized social media to amplify the voices of marginalized communities and advocate for racial justice.

The ability of social media to mobilize large groups of people around a shared cause has made it a force to be reckoned with. Hashtags, viral challenges and online petitions have become common tools for activism, enabling individuals to participate in social change from the comfort of their own homes.

The Dark Side of Social Media Storytelling

While social media has undoubtedly revolutionized storytelling, it is not without its drawbacks. The emphasis on visual content and short-form narratives can lead to a superficiality of storytelling, where complex issues are reduced to sound bites and clickbait headlines.

Moreover, the algorithmic nature of social media platforms can create echo chambers, where users are only exposed to content that aligns with their existing beliefs. This can lead to a polarization of opinions and a decline in civil discourse.

Additionally, the spread of misinformation and fake news on social media has become a major concern. The ease with which false narratives can be disseminated and amplified can have serious consequences, eroding trust in institutions and undermining democratic processes.

The Future of Social Media Storytelling

Despite the challenges, social media continues to evolve and shape the way we tell stories. The rise of new platforms like Clubhouse, which focuses on audio-based storytelling, suggests that the future of social media storytelling is likely to be multifaceted and dynamic.

As technology advances, we can expect to see even more innovative ways to tell stories on social media. Virtual reality, augmented reality and artificial intelligence are just some of the technologies that have the potential to revolutionize the way we create and consume stories.

Embracing the Potential of Social Media Storytelling

For individuals and brands alike, social media offers a wealth of opportunities for storytelling. By understanding the nuances of each platform and tailoring content to specific audiences, it is possible to create compelling narratives that resonate with people on a deep level.

However, it is important to be mindful of the potential pitfalls of social media storytelling. By prioritizing authenticity, accuracy and diversity of perspectives, we can ensure that social media remains a powerful tool for positive change.

In the words of author Neil Gaiman, 'Stories are the most important thing in the world. Without stories, we wouldn't be human beings at all.' As we navigate the ever-evolving landscape of social media, let us embrace the power of storytelling to connect, inspire and transform our world.

16

ENHANCING STORYTELLING SKILLS

Enhancing your storytelling skills is a worthwhile pursuit, as stories have the power to captivate, inform and inspire. Whether you're looking to improve your personal narratives, professional presentations or written communication, there are various techniques and resources available to help you on your journey.

Practice and Feedback

'The difference between ordinary and extraordinary is practice.'

—Vladimir Horowitz

Practice and feedback are the conductor's baton and the discerning ear of the audience. They are the twin pillars upon which the edifice of mastery is built. Horowitz, a virtuoso pianist, understood the transformative power of relentless practice. In the realm of storytelling, this principle holds equally true.

The Practice Arena: Where Stories Take Flight

Practice is not merely repetition; it is the deliberate, focused refinement of your craft. It is the arena where your stories take flight, where characters come to life and where the rhythm of your narrative finds its cadence.

- **Embrace the Power of Repetition:** Like a musician rehearsing a complex piece, the storyteller must rehearse their tales. Tell your stories to friends, family, colleagues or even to yourself in the mirror. Each retelling is an opportunity to refine your delivery, experiment with different phrasings and discover new nuances in your narrative.
- **Seek Out Diverse Audiences:** Just as a play is tested before a live audience, your stories benefit from being shared with diverse groups. Each audience brings a unique perspective, and their reactions provide valuable insights into the strengths and weaknesses of your storytelling.

- **Record and Review:** In the digital age, recording yourself telling a story is as easy as pressing a button. This simple act can be incredibly revealing. By watching or listening to your performance, you can identify areas for improvement in your pacing, tone, body language and overall delivery.

- **Experiment with Different Formats:** Storytelling is not confined to the spoken word. Experiment with writing your stories down, creating visual narratives through drawings or photographs or even crafting short films. Each format offers a unique set of challenges and rewards, and exploring different mediums can expand your storytelling repertoire.

- **Join a Storytelling Group or Workshop:** The camaraderie and shared passion of a storytelling community can be incredibly motivating. By joining a group or workshop, you gain access to a supportive network of fellow storytellers who can offer encouragement, feedback and inspiration.

The Feedback Loop: A Compass for Growth

Feedback is the compass that guides your storytelling journey. It illuminates the path towards improvement, highlighting areas of strength and revealing growth opportunities.

- **Be Open to Feedback:** The first step in receiving valuable feedback is to be open to it. This means setting aside your ego and approaching feedback with a willingness to learn and grow. Remember, feedback is not a personal attack; it is a gift that can help you become a better storyteller.

- **Ask Specific Questions:** Don't just ask, 'How was my story?' Instead, seek out specific feedback on particular aspects of your storytelling. For example, you might ask, 'Was the pacing too slow or too fast?' or 'Did the characters feel believable?'

- **Seek Feedback from Diverse Sources:** Don't limit yourself to feedback from friends and family. Seek out feedback from experienced storytellers, teachers, mentors or even strangers. The more diverse your sources of feedback, the richer and more comprehensive your understanding of your strengths and weaknesses will be.

- **Give Feedback Gracefully:** Remember, feedback is a two-way street. When offering feedback to others, do so with kindness and respect. Focus on specific aspects of their storytelling and offer constructive suggestions for improvement.

- **Create a Feedback Ritual:** Make feedback a regular part of your storytelling practice. Set aside time each week to review feedback you've received, and to reflect on how you can incorporate it into your storytelling.

The Alchemy of Practice and Feedback

The alchemy of practice and feedback lies in their synergistic relationship. Practice hones your skills, while feedback illuminates the path towards mastery. By embracing both, you embark on a continuous cycle of growth and refinement.

Storytelling is a journey, not a destination. There is always room for improvement, always new stories to tell and always new ways to connect with your audience.

Learning from Master Storytellers

In storytelling, where imagination reigns supreme and emotions intertwine, master storytellers have emerged as beacons of inspiration and knowledge. Their ability to transport us to distant lands, introduce us to unforgettable characters and evoke a kaleidoscope of feelings is nothing short of extraordinary.

The Art of Observation

One of the most fundamental traits shared by master storytellers is their keen sense of observation. They possess an uncanny ability to perceive the intricacies of human behaviour, the nuances of social interactions and the subtleties of the natural world. By immersing themselves in their surroundings, they gather a wealth of material that serves as the bedrock of their narratives.

Consider the works of Jane Austen, renowned for her insightful portrayals of English society in the early nineteenth century. Her novels, such as *Pride and Prejudice* and *Emma*, are replete with detailed descriptions of social customs, manners and the dynamics of relationships. Austen's meticulous observations allowed her to create vivid characters that resonate with readers even today.

The short stories of Anton Chekhov, a master of realism, are rich in observations of ordinary life in Russia during the late nineteenth century. Chekhov's stories, such as *The Lady with the Dog* and *The Bet*, offer glimpses into the lives of doctors, lawyers, merchants and peasants, capturing their hopes, fears and desires with remarkable clarity.

The Power of Empathy

Another hallmark of master storytellers is their profound sense of empathy. They possess the ability to step into the shoes of their characters, understand their motivations and feel their joys and sorrows. This deep connection with their characters allows them to craft narratives that are both compelling and emotionally resonant.

Harper Lee's *To Kill a Mockingbird* is a prime example of a story that is fuelled by empathy. Through the eyes of

Scout Finch, a young girl growing up in the racially charged South of the 1930s, Lee explores themes of prejudice, injustice and compassion. Scout's innocence and sense of fairness make her a relatable character, and her journey of understanding the complexities of the world around her is a powerful testament to the importance of empathy.

Chimamanda Ngozi Adichie's novels, such as *Half of a Yellow Sun* and *Americanah*, are characterized by their deep empathy for their characters. Adichie's stories explore the complexities of identity, race and belonging, and her ability to inhabit the minds of her characters from diverse backgrounds is a testament to her empathy and understanding.

The Mastery of Language

Master storytellers are also masters of language. They possess a deep understanding of grammar, syntax and vocabulary, and they use this knowledge to craft narratives that are both elegant and evocative. Their words paint vivid pictures in our minds, their sentences flow with rhythm and grace and their paragraphs build to emotional crescendos.

Consider the works of Gabriel García Márquez, a Nobel laureate in literature. Márquez's novels, such as *One Hundred Years of Solitude* and *Love in the Time of Cholera*, are celebrated for their lyrical prose, their magical realism and their exploration of the human condition. Márquez's mastery of language allows him to create worlds that are both familiar and fantastical, and his characters linger in our memories long after we've finished reading.

The poetry of Maya Angelou, a celebrated American author and activist, is characterized by its rhythmic beauty, its emotional power and its exploration of themes of race, gender and identity. Angelou's poems, such as *Still I Rise* and *Phenomenal Woman*, are anthems of hope, resilience and self-love, and their words continue to inspire and uplift readers around the world.

The Importance of Revision

Master storytellers understand the importance of revision. They know that the first draft of a story is rarely the best, and they are willing to put in the time and effort to refine their work. They are not afraid to cut out unnecessary scenes, to add new details and to experiment with different approaches.

Ernest Hemingway, a Nobel laureate in literature, was known for his rigorous revision process. He famously said, 'The first draft of anything is shit,' and he would often revise his stories multiple times before he was satisfied. Hemingway's dedication to revision allowed him to craft narratives that were spare, precise and impactful.

Learning from master storytellers is an invaluable endeavour for anyone who aspires to improve their own storytelling skills. By observing the world around us, cultivating empathy for our characters, mastering the art of language and embracing the process of revision, we can all become better storytellers and create narratives that captivate and inspire our audiences.

Adapting Stories for Different Mediums

'The heart of storytelling remains the same, whether you're etching words on parchment or pixels on a screen. But the tools, the language, the very rhythm of the narrative must evolve with each new medium.'

—Unknown

The art of adaptation has become a critical skill. With platforms ranging from the printed page to the silver screen, podcasts, video games and the virtual realm, a story's potential is no longer confined to a single format. The ability to metamorphose a narrative, preserving its essence while tailoring it to the unique demands of each medium, is a hallmark of a versatile storyteller.

The Alchemy of Adaptation

Adaptation is not merely a matter of transferring words from one format to another; it's a process akin to alchemy, where the raw material of a story is transmuted into new forms, each with its own distinct properties. A successful adaptation requires a deep understanding of both the original story and the target medium, as well as a willingness to experiment and innovate.

The Printed Page: The Foundation of Storytelling

The written word, whether in the form of a novel, short story or comic book, is the bedrock of narrative art. It's here that the storyteller has the most freedom to explore character, theme and plot, unencumbered by the constraints of time, budget or technology.

However, the written word also demands a high level of craft, as the storyteller must rely solely on language to create vivid imagery, engaging dialogue and a compelling plot.

The Silver Screen: A Visual Symphony

Film is a visual medium, where the story is told through images, sound and movement. This presents both opportunities and challenges for the storyteller.

On the one hand, film can bring a story to life in a way that no other medium can, immersing the audience in a world of sight and sound. On the other hand, the visual nature of film can also limit the storyteller's ability to explore character and theme in depth, as the focus is often on action and spectacle.

The Stage: Where Stories Come Alive

The theatre is a live medium, where the story unfolds in real time before a live audience. This creates a unique energy and intimacy that is difficult to replicate in other formats. However, theatre also has its limitations, as the storyteller must work within the confines of a physical stage and a fixed performance time.

Podcasts: The Theatre of the Mind

Podcasts are a relatively new medium, but they have quickly become a popular platform for storytelling. The audio-only format of podcasts allows the storyteller to focus on character, dialogue and sound design, creating a rich and immersive experience for the listener.

Video Games: Interactive Narratives

Video games are a unique form of storytelling, as they allow the audience to actively participate in the narrative. This interactivity opens up a whole new realm of possibilities for storytelling, but it also presents new challenges, as the storyteller must create a narrative that is both engaging and flexible enough to accommodate the player's choices.

The Virtual Realm: A New Frontier

Virtual reality (VR) is the newest frontier in storytelling, offering a fully immersive experience that blurs the lines between the real and the virtual. VR has the potential to revolutionize the way we tell and experience stories, but it is still in its early stages of development, and the full extent of its impact on storytelling remains to be seen.

The Storyteller's Toolkit

Adapting a story for different mediums requires a versatile toolkit. Here are a few essential tools that every storyteller should have in their arsenal:

- **Understanding of the Target Medium:** Each medium has its own unique strengths and weaknesses. Successful adaptation requires a deep understanding of the target medium so that the storyteller can leverage its strengths and mitigate its weaknesses.
- **Flexibility and Adaptability:** The process of adaptation is often one of trial and error. The storyteller must be willing to experiment, try new

things and adapt to the unique demands of each medium.

- **Collaboration:** Adaptation is rarely a solo endeavour. It often involves collaboration with other creatives, such as screenwriters, directors, actors and designers. The ability to collaborate effectively is essential for a successful adaptation.
- **Respect for the Original Story:** While adaptation requires change, it's important to respect the essence of the original story. A successful adaptation honours the original while bringing something new to the table.
- **A Willingness to Take Risks:** Adaptation is not about playing it safe. It's about pushing boundaries, experimenting with new ideas and taking risks. The most successful adaptations are often the ones that take the biggest risks.

The art of adaptation is a complex and ever-evolving one. But for storytellers who are willing to embrace the challenge, the rewards can be immense. By adapting their stories for different mediums, storytellers can reach new audiences, expand the reach of their narratives and create truly immersive and unforgettable experiences.

PART IV

INTEGRATING
SKILLS IN DAILY LIFE

17

COMBINING QUESTIONING, CONFIDENCE AND STORYTELLING

The art of conversation is a subtle dance, a delicate interplay of words, emotions and ideas. It's a skill that can unlock doors, forge connections and propel you towards professional success. But what truly sets apart a master conversationalist?

It's the ability to seamlessly weave together three essential elements: questioning, confidence and storytelling.

The Interplay Between the Three Skills

> *'The most powerful person in the world is the storyteller. The storyteller sets the vision, values, and agenda of an entire generation that is to come.'*
>
> —Steve Jobs

In a world that's constantly vying for our attention, the ability to influence—to truly connect with others and inspire action—is a superpower.

At the heart of this superpower lies an intricate dance between three fundamental skills: the art of questioning, the unwavering strength of confidence and the timeless allure of storytelling.

The Art of Questioning: A Catalyst for Connection

Questions are the lifeblood of any meaningful interaction. They invite curiosity, foster deeper understanding and create a space for genuine connection. In the realm of influence, questions are not merely tools for gathering information; they are instruments for sparking thought, challenging assumptions and illuminating new perspectives.

Consider the Socratic method, a timeless approach to learning and critical thinking. By posing a series of carefully crafted questions, Socrates was able to guide his students towards profound insights and self-discovery. This method, when wielded with skill and intention, can be a powerful tool for influencing others.

The Strength of Confidence: A Foundation for Influence

Confidence is the bedrock upon which influence is built. It is the unshakable belief in oneself, one's ideas and one's ability to make a difference. When we speak with confidence, our words carry weight and conviction. When we act with confidence, our actions inspire trust and respect.

Confidence is not about arrogance or bravado; it is about quiet self-assurance and a deep-rooted belief in one's own value. It is the courage to speak up, stand out and challenge the status quo. When we cultivate confidence, we become beacons of influence, drawing others towards our vision and inspiring them to action.

The Allure of Storytelling: A Gateway to Influence

Stories are the universal language of the human experience. They transport us to other worlds, ignite our imaginations and evoke powerful emotions. In the realm of influence, stories are not merely forms of entertainment; they are vehicles for transmitting values, inspiring action and shaping beliefs.

Consider the impact of Martin Luther King Jr's 'I Have a Dream' speech. Through his powerful storytelling, he was able to galvanize a nation and propel the Civil Rights Movement forward. This is the power of storytelling—it can move hearts, change minds and ignite revolutions.

The Interplay: Where Questions Meet Confidence and Ignite Stories

The true power of influence lies in the interplay between these three skills. When we master the art of questioning, we gain deeper insights into the needs, desires and motivations of others. This understanding allows us to tailor our communication and influence strategies more effectively.

When we cultivate unwavering confidence, we project an aura of authority and credibility. Our words and actions become more persuasive, and we can inspire others to follow our lead.

When we harness the power of storytelling, we tap into the deepest emotions and aspirations of our audience. Our messages become more memorable, impactful and transformative.

Together, these three skills create a powerful alchemy of influence. They allow us to connect with others on a deeper level, inspire action and, ultimately, make a meaningful difference in the world.

The Power of Combining Questioning, Confidence and Storytelling

When we combine questioning, confidence and storytelling, we create a potent formula for influence. Questions open doors to understanding, confidence bolsters our message and stories make our ideas unforgettable.

- **Questioning to Understand:** By asking insightful questions, we gain a deeper understanding of our audience's needs, desires and pain points. This allows us to tailor our message to resonate with them on a personal level.
- **Confidence to Persuade:** When we speak with confidence, our words carry weight and conviction. We project an aura of authority and credibility, making our message more persuasive.
- **Storytelling to Inspire:** Stories are powerful tools for inspiring action. They tap into our emotions, making our ideas more memorable and impactful. When we share stories that resonate with our audience, we can motivate them to take action and achieve their goals.

By mastering these three skills and weaving them together, we can unlock our full potential as influencers. We can connect with others on a deeper level, inspire action and, ultimately, make a lasting impact on the world.

Practical Exercises for Daily Practice

'The unexamined life is not worth living.'

—Socrates

Socrates, the father of Western philosophy, emphasized the importance of self-reflection and questioning. This chapter dives deep into practical exercises designed to infuse your daily life with the power of inquiry, bolster your confidence and enhance your storytelling abilities. These are not merely abstract concepts; they are skills that, with practice, can transform how you interact with the world and yourself.

1. The Morning Question

Begin your day with a single, open-ended question. It could be about anything that sparks your curiosity: a current event, a personal challenge or a philosophical quandary. Write it down and let your mind wander. This practice primes your brain for a day of active engagement and critical thinking. Research shows that individuals who engage in regular self-questioning demonstrate higher levels of creativity and problem-solving skills.

2. The Confidence Booster

Identify one small action that you can take today that aligns with your values and goals. It could be as simple as making your bed, completing a work task or reaching out to a friend. The act of accomplishment, no matter how minor, releases dopamine, a neurotransmitter associated with pleasure and motivation. This positive reinforcement strengthens your belief in your abilities. Studies indicate that even small wins can significantly boost self-efficacy and resilience.

3.   The Storyteller's Lens

Throughout your day, pay attention to the narratives unfolding around you. It could be a conversation overheard at the coffee shop, a news headline or an interaction with a colleague. Consider the different perspectives, motivations and emotions involved. Practise retelling these stories, either to yourself or to others, focusing on the details that resonate with you. This exercise sharpens your observation skills and your ability to connect with others through shared experiences. Research suggests that storytelling is a fundamental human need that fosters social bonding and empathy.

4.   The Evening Reflection

Before you retire for the night, take a few moments to review your day. What were the highlights? What challenges did you face? What questions did you ask? What stories did you encounter? Write down your thoughts and feelings. This practice not only helps you process your experiences but also provides valuable insights into your patterns of thought and behaviour. Studies have shown that journalling can reduce stress, improve mood and enhance self-awareness.

5. The Weekly Challenge

Once a week, step outside your comfort zone and try something new. It could be a new hobby, a new cuisine or a new social activity. Embrace the uncertainty and opportunity for growth. This practice expands your horizons and helps you build resilience in the face of the unknown. Research indicates that individuals who regularly engage in novel experiences exhibit greater adaptability and openness to change.

6. The Monthly Review

At the end of each month, reflect on your progress. Have you become more curious? More confident? A better storyteller? What have you learnt about yourself? What areas would you like to focus on next? This practice helps you stay on track and celebrate your achievements. Studies have shown that setting and reviewing goals is crucial for personal and professional development.

7. The Yearly Reset

Take some time at the beginning of each year to set intentions for the months ahead. What do you want to achieve? What kind of person do you want to become? Write down your aspirations and create a plan for how you will work towards them. This practice gives you a sense of direction and purpose. Research suggests that individuals who set meaningful goals are more likely to experience a sense of fulfilment and well-being.

The exercises outlined in this chapter are not a one-size-fits-all solution. Experiment, adapt and find what works best for you. Remember, the goal is not perfection but progress. The key is consistency and commitment. By integrating these practices into your daily routine, you can unlock your full potential and live a more meaningful and fulfilling life.

Additional Tips

- Find a supportive community or accountability partner to share your journey with.
- Celebrate your successes, no matter how small.
- Be patient with yourself. Change takes time and effort.
- Don't be afraid to seek professional guidance if you need it.

Remember, the path to self-improvement is a lifelong journey. Embrace the challenges and enjoy the rewards.

18

CASE STUDIES AND
REAL-LIFE EXAMPLES

The art of storytelling isn't merely reserved for campfires and bedtime tales. It's a potent tool in the professional realm, capable of forging connections, inspiring action and driving success. In the world of work, where facts and figures often dominate, stories breathe life into ideas, making them memorable and impactful. They create an emotional resonance that data alone cannot achieve.

Successful Applications in Personal Life

'The only person you are destined to become is the person you decide to be.'

—Ralph Waldo Emerson

Introduction

This chapter ventures into the heart of personal transformation, where the principles of integrating skills in daily life manifest in remarkable ways. While previous chapters explored skill integration in various contexts, this chapter delves into the profound impact it has on individual lives. Through compelling real-life examples and case studies, we'll witness how individuals have harnessed integrated skills to achieve personal goals, overcome challenges and cultivate a life of purpose and fulfilment.

Case Study 1: A Journey of Self-Discovery and Career Reinvention

Meet Sarah, a former corporate executive who found herself at a crossroads in her career. Feeling unfulfilled and disconnected from her work, Sarah embarked on a journey of self-discovery. She began exploring her interests and passions outside of her corporate role, taking up painting, volunteering at a local community centre and attending workshops on personal development.

Through these experiences, Sarah began to integrate her diverse skills and experiences. She realized that her organizational skills from the corporate world could be applied to her volunteer work, while her newfound creativity could be expressed through painting. This integration of skills led to a profound shift in Sarah's perspective.

Inspired by her newfound passions and skills, Sarah decided to leave her corporate job and pursue a career in the non-profit sector. She leveraged her integrated skills to land a fulfilling role as a programme director at a local organization, where she could combine her passion for helping others with her organizational and leadership abilities.

Case Study 2: Building Stronger Relationships Through Effective Communication

John and Emily, a married couple struggling with communication issues, found themselves on the brink of separation. They frequently argued, misunderstood each other's intentions and felt increasingly distant. In a desperate attempt to salvage their relationship, they sought couples therapy.

Through therapy, John and Emily learnt the importance of active listening, empathy and non-violent communication. They practised expressing their needs and feelings clearly and respectfully, while also actively listening to each other's perspectives. As they integrated these communication skills into their daily interactions, they noticed a significant improvement in their relationship.

Arguments became less frequent and less heated, replaced by productive conversations. They felt more connected and understood each other on a deeper level. Their newfound communication skills not only saved their marriage but also strengthened their bond, allowing them to build a more loving and supportive partnership.

Case Study 3: Overcoming Personal Challenges Through Resilience and Resourcefulness

Mark, a young man who had been struggling with depression and anxiety for years, felt trapped in a cycle of negativity and despair. He had difficulty maintaining relationships, holding down a job and finding joy in life. Desperate for a change, Mark sought professional help and began a journey of healing and personal growth.

Through therapy, Mark learnt about the importance of self-care, mindfulness and cognitive restructuring. He practised challenging negative thoughts, focusing on his strengths and building healthy coping mechanisms. As he integrated these skills into his daily life, Mark noticed a gradual but significant improvement in his mental health.

He started exercising regularly, eating healthier and engaging in activities that brought him joy. He reconnected with friends and family, found a fulfilling job and began to feel more hopeful about the future. Mark's journey of overcoming personal challenges demonstrates the power of resilience and resourcefulness, skills that can be cultivated and integrated into daily life to create positive change.

Real-Life Examples of Integrated Skills in Action

Beyond these case studies, countless individuals have found success by integrating skills in their personal lives. A single mother might leverage her time management and organizational skills to balance work, parenting and personal pursuits. An aspiring artist could utilize their creativity and technical skills to produce stunning works of art. A recent graduate might combine their communication and interpersonal skills to land their dream job.

The examples are endless, as the possibilities for integrating skills are as diverse as the individuals who employ them. In each instance, the integration of skills catalyses personal growth, enabling individuals to achieve their goals, overcome challenges and create a life that is both meaningful and fulfilling.

The successful application of integrated skills in personal life is a testament to the power of human potential. By identifying, developing and combining their diverse skills and experiences, individuals can unlock new possibilities, navigate challenges and create a life of purpose and fulfilment.

Impactful Uses in Professional Settings

> *'The illiterate of the twenty-first century will not be those who cannot read and write, but those who cannot learn, unlearn and relearn.'*
>
> —Alvin Toffler

Toffler's prophetic words ring truer than ever in today's rapidly evolving professional landscape. The integration of diverse skills, once considered a luxury, has become a necessity for thriving in the modern workplace. The ability to learn, adapt and combine seemingly disparate skill sets is the key to unlocking new opportunities, solving complex problems and driving innovation. This chapter delves into real-world examples and case studies that illuminate the transformative power of skill integration in professional settings.

A Multifaceted Approach to Leadership

In the realm of leadership, the integration of soft and hard skills is paramount. Leaders who possess technical expertise but lack emotional intelligence or communication skills often struggle to inspire and motivate their teams. Conversely, leaders with exceptional interpersonal skills but limited technical knowledge may find it challenging to make informed decisions or gain the respect of their colleagues.

Consider the case of a software engineering manager who, despite their technical brilliance, was struggling to foster collaboration and creativity within their team. By integrating their technical skills with active listening, empathy and conflict resolution techniques, the manager was able to create a more supportive and inclusive environment, leading to increased productivity and employee satisfaction.

The Art of Persuasion: Bridging the Gap Between Data and Emotion

In fields such as marketing, sales and public relations, the ability to persuade and influence is essential. This involves not only understanding the target audience and crafting compelling messages but also integrating analytical skills to measure the effectiveness of campaigns and make data-driven adjustments.

A pharmaceutical sales representative, for instance, must not only possess in-depth knowledge of their products but also be able to establish a rapport with healthcare professionals, understand their needs and present information in a way that resonates both emotionally and intellectually. By integrating scientific knowledge with interpersonal skills and data analysis, the sales representative can effectively communicate the value of their products and drive sales growth.

Innovation at the Intersection of Disciplines

Innovation often arises from the integration of diverse perspectives and skill sets. In industries such as technology, healthcare and environmental science, the ability to combine knowledge from different disciplines is crucial for developing novel solutions to complex challenges.

A team of researchers working on a new drug delivery system, for example, might include chemists, biologists, engineers and clinicians. By integrating their expertise, the team can design a system that is not only effective but also safe, affordable and user-friendly. Similarly, in the field of renewable energy, engineers, environmental scientists and economists must collaborate to develop sustainable solutions that are both technologically feasible and economically viable.

The Lifelong Learner: Embracing Continuous Growth and Development

The most successful professionals are those who embrace lifelong learning. This involves not only staying abreast of the latest developments in one's field but also actively seeking out opportunities to acquire new skills and knowledge.

A financial analyst, for instance, might enrol in a course on data science to enhance their ability to analyse market trends and make informed investment decisions. An accountant might pursue a certification in project management to expand their career options and take on more challenging roles. By continuously learning and expanding their skill set, professionals can remain competitive in the job market and adapt to the ever-changing demands of their industries.

The Future of Work: A Call for Adaptability and Resilience

The integration of skills is not only a matter of personal and professional growth but also a matter of survival in the modern workplace. As automation and artificial intelligence continue to transform industries, the jobs of the future will require a combination of technical, interpersonal and cognitive skills.

To thrive in this new era of work, professionals must be adaptable, resilient and willing to embrace change. This means not only acquiring new skills but also cultivating a growth mindset and a willingness to step outside of one's comfort zone. The ability to learn, unlearn and relearn will be the defining characteristic of a successful professional in the twenty-first century.

19

DEVELOPING A PERSONAL ACTION PLAN

A personal action plan is more than just a to-do list; it's a road map for your aspirations, a blueprint for your dreams and a compass guiding you towards your desired destination. It's a structured approach to self-improvement, helping you identify where you are, where you want to be and how to get there. It involves setting clear goals, breaking them down into actionable tasks and tracking your progress.

Setting Goals for Improvement

'The purpose of setting goals is to win the game. The purpose of building a team is to make sure there is a game to win.'

—Bill Walsh

Goals serve as our guiding stars, illuminating the path towards our desired future. They provide a sense of direction, purpose and motivation, propelling us forward even when faced with challenges.

The process of setting goals, however, is not merely about jotting down aspirations on a piece of paper; it requires thoughtful consideration, careful planning and unwavering commitment. In essence, it's about crafting a road map for personal growth and transformation.

Understanding the Power of Goals

Goals are not just abstract wishes; they are concrete targets that we strive to achieve. They can range from small, short-term objectives to ambitious, long-term aspirations. Regardless of their scale, goals play a pivotal role in personal development by providing a number of key benefits:

- **Direction and Focus:** Goals give us a clear sense of where we're headed and what we need to do to get there. They help us avoid distractions and stay on track, even when faced with setbacks or obstacles.
- **Motivation and Drive:** Goals provide a powerful source of motivation. When we have a clear vision of what we want to achieve, we're more likely to take action and persevere in the face of challenges.

- **Self-Efficacy and Confidence:** As we achieve our goals, we build self-efficacy—the belief in our ability to succeed. This, in turn, boosts our confidence and empowers us to take on even bigger challenges.
- **Personal Growth and Development:** Goals push us beyond our comfort zones, encouraging us to learn new skills, develop new habits and expand our knowledge and understanding.
- **Sense of Accomplishment and Fulfilment:** Achieving our goals brings a deep sense of satisfaction and fulfilment. It reinforces our commitment to personal development and motivates us to continue striving for improvement.

Setting Smart Goals

To maximize the effectiveness of goal setting, it's crucial to set SMART goals. SMART is an acronym that stands for:

- **Specific:** Your goals should be clear and well-defined. Avoid vague statements like 'I want to be healthier'. Instead, be specific about what you want to achieve, such as 'I want to lose ten pounds in three months'.
- **Measurable:** Your goals should be quantifiable so you can track your progress and determine whether you're on track. For example, instead of saying, 'I want

to read more', set a measurable goal like 'I want to read one book per month'.

- **Achievable:** Your goals should be realistic and attainable, given your current resources and capabilities. Don't set yourself up for failure by setting goals that are too ambitious or unrealistic.
- **Relevant:** Your goals should be aligned with your values, interests and overall life goals. Don't set goals simply because you think you should; choose goals that are meaningful and relevant to you.
- **Time-Bound:** Your goals should have a specific deadline or timeframe for completion. This creates a sense of urgency and helps you stay motivated and focused.

The Role of Personal Action Plans

While setting SMART goals is a crucial first step, it's equally important to develop a personal action plan to guide your efforts. A personal action plan is a detailed road map that outlines the specific steps you need to take to achieve your goals. It includes:

- **Specific Actions:** Break down your goals into smaller, more manageable tasks. For example, if your goal is to lose ten pounds, your action plan might include specific actions like exercising for thirty minutes five days a week, tracking your food intake and reducing your calorie intake by 500 calories per day.

- **Timeline:** Assign deadlines or timeframes to each action step. This helps you stay on track and ensures that you're making progress towards your goals.
- **Resources:** Identify the resources you need to complete each action step. This might include things like gym memberships, healthy cookbooks or the support of a personal trainer or nutritionist.
- **Obstacles and Solutions:** Anticipate potential obstacles or challenges that might arise and develop strategies for overcoming them. For example, if you anticipate that you might have trouble sticking to your exercise routine, you could develop a plan for staying motivated, such as finding a workout buddy or rewarding yourself for reaching milestones.
- **Review and Revision:** Regularly review your personal action plan and make adjustments as needed. Your goals and circumstances might change over time, so it's important to be flexible and adaptable.

Key Strategies for Goal Achievement

In addition to setting SMART goals and developing a personal action plan, there are a number of key strategies that can help you achieve your goals:

- **Visualize Success:** Imagine yourself achieving your goals in vivid detail. This can help you stay motivated and focused, especially when faced with challenges.

- **Break Down Goals into Smaller Steps:** Don't be overwhelmed by the scale of your goals. Break them down into smaller, more manageable steps that you can tackle one at a time.

- **Track Your Progress:** Regularly track your progress towards your goals. This can help you identify areas where you're excelling and areas where you might need to make adjustments.

- **Celebrate Your Successes:** Take the time to celebrate your successes, no matter how small they may seem. This can help you stay motivated and reinforce your commitment to your goals.

- **Don't Give Up:** There will be setbacks and challenges along the way. Don't let them discourage you. Learn from your mistakes, adjust your approach and keep moving forward.

By setting SMART goals, developing a personal action plan and employing these key strategies, you can unlock your full potential and achieve the personal growth and transformation you desire. Remember, the journey of a thousand miles begins with a single step. Start by setting your goals today and take that first step towards a brighter future.

Tracking Progress and Reflecting on Growth

'The unexamined life is not worth living.'

—Socrates

As you embark on the journey of personal development, armed with your meticulously crafted Personal Action Plan, the wisdom of Socrates's words rings true. It's not enough to simply set goals and initiate action; the true essence of growth lies in the ongoing process of tracking progress and reflecting on the path travelled. This chapter delves into the indispensable tools of tracking and reflection, illuminating how they serve as the compass and the mirror, respectively, guiding you towards your desired destination while providing insights into your evolving self.

Progress Tracking: Charting the Course

Imagine setting sail on a vast ocean without a compass or map. You might drift aimlessly, uncertain of your direction or how far you've come. Similarly, in the realm of personal development, tracking progress acts as your navigational instrument, providing a clear sense of direction and distance travelled. By quantifying your achievements and milestones, you gain a tangible measure of your growth, bolstering your motivation and reinforcing the effectiveness of your Personal Action Plan.

The methods for tracking progress are as diverse as the goals they measure. For fitness objectives, it might involve logging workouts, tracking body measurements or noting improvements in strength or endurance. In the realm of professional development, progress might be gauged by the completion of courses, acquisition of new skills or advancement in your career. Financial goals might be tracked through savings targets, debt reduction or investment growth.

Regardless of the specific method, the key is to establish clear metrics and consistently record your progress. Consider using a journal, spreadsheet or specialized app to create a visual representation of your journey. Graphs, charts and timelines can be powerful tools for illustrating your advancement over time. As you witness the tangible evidence of your efforts, your confidence will soar, propelling you forward with renewed determination.

Reflection: Illuminating the Path

While progress tracking illuminates the external markers of your journey, reflection delves into the internal landscape, shedding light on your thoughts, feelings and motivations. It serves as a mirror, reflecting your evolving self and revealing the deeper meaning behind your actions. By taking the time to pause and introspect, you gain valuable insights into your strengths, weaknesses and areas for further growth.

Reflection can take many forms, from journalling and meditation to conversations with trusted friends or mentors. The key is to create a space where you can honestly assess your experiences and emotions. Ask yourself probing questions:

- What have I learnt from my successes and setbacks?
- How have my goals and values evolved over time?
- What obstacles have I encountered, and how have I overcome them?
- What am I most proud of?
- What areas do I still need to work on?

By engaging in this self-inquiry, you cultivate self-awareness, a cornerstone of personal development. As you understand your motivations and patterns of behaviour, you gain the power to make conscious choices that align with your deepest aspirations.

The Synergy of Tracking and Reflection

Tracking progress and reflecting on growth are not isolated activities; they are intertwined aspects of a dynamic process.

As you track your progress, you gather data that informs your reflections. Your reflections, in turn, can lead to adjustments in your Personal Action Plan, ensuring that your actions remain aligned with your evolving goals and values.

This continuous feedback loop is essential for sustained growth. It allows you to course-correct when necessary, celebrate your achievements and learn from your mistakes. By embracing both tracking and reflection, you create a powerful synergy that propels you towards your full potential.

Practical Strategies for Tracking Progress and Reflecting on Growth

Here are some practical strategies to integrate tracking and reflection into your personal development journey:

- **Set SMART Goals:** Ensure your goals are Specific, Measurable, Achievable, Relevant and Time-Bound. This provides a clear framework for tracking progress.
- **Choose Your Tools:** Select tracking tools that resonate with you. Whether it's a journal, app or spreadsheet, find a method that you enjoy and will consistently use.
- **Schedule Regular Check-Ins:** Set aside dedicated time for reflection. This could be daily, weekly or monthly, depending on your preferences and goals.
- **Ask Powerful Questions:** During reflection, delve deep with thought-provoking questions that challenge your assumptions and spark insights.

- **Celebrate Your Wins:** Acknowledge your achievements, no matter how small. This reinforces positive behaviour and fuels motivation.
- **Embrace Setbacks as Learning Opportunities:** Don't be discouraged by setbacks. Analyse what went wrong, extract the lessons and move forward with renewed determination.
- **Seek Support:** Share your progress and reflections with trusted friends, mentors or a coach. They can provide valuable feedback and encouragement.

The Journey Continues

As you continue your personal development journey, remember that tracking progress and reflecting on growth are not merely tasks to be completed; they are lifelong practices that empower you to take ownership of your path. By honing these skills, you transform into a conscious architect of your own destiny, equipped with the tools to navigate the complexities of life and create a future that reflects your deepest aspirations.

CONCLUSION

Mastering questioning, confidence and storytelling is an ongoing journey. Embrace lifelong learning and continuously seek opportunities to refine these skills. Remember that there is always room for growth and improvement, no matter how much experience you have.

As you continue to develop your questioning, confidence and storytelling skills, make sure to apply what you've learnt in real-life situations. Whether it's during a presentation or a conversation with colleagues, take the time to implement these techniques and assess their effectiveness. This will help solidify your understanding and identify areas for further improvement.

Personal development is a lifelong pursuit. Integrate these skills into your daily life and professional interactions to enhance your communication and build stronger connections.

By mastering the art of asking questions, building confidence and telling compelling stories, you can elevate your professional and personal interactions. Start your journey today and unlock the full potential of your communication skills. So, keep practising and refining these skills and embrace the continuous process of growth. As you integrate questioning, confidence and storytelling into your communication style, you will see positive results in all aspects of your life. Remember to be open to feedback and always seek opportunities to learn and improve. With dedication and determination, you can become a master communicator.

Thank you for reading this guide on mastering questioning, confidence and storytelling. We hope it has provided valuable insights and practical tips that you can apply in all areas of your life. Keep questioning, keep building your confidence and keep telling captivating stories! Now, go out there and communicate with impact! Happy communicating!

Scan QR code to access the
Penguin Random House India website